THE WAY OF THE LAMB

THE WAY
OF THE LAMB

The Spirit of Childhood and the End of the Age

JOHN SAWARD

IGNATIUS PRESS   SAN FRANCISCO

Typeset by Waverley Typesetters, Galashiels
Printed and bound in Great Britain by Biddles Ltd, Guildford

Contents

Acknowledgements

This book on childhood was a gift to me from my own children. The research has been pursued for over twenty years, but the title and chief motif were suggested three years ago by my youngest daughter, Anna. With all my heart I dedicate everything that follows to her. 'Out of the mouth of infants and of sucklings thou hast perfected praise, because of thy enemies, that thou mayest destroy the enemy and the avenger' (Ps. 8:3).

Solemnity of St Joseph
19 March 1999

Abbreviations

ET   English translation

THE WORKS OF ST THÉRÈSE

CJ   *Carnet jaune* of Mother Agnès
DE   *Derniers entretiens*
LT   *Lettres*
MS A, B, C   The three autobiographical manuscripts (original
                      pagination indicated by '1r' etc.)
OC   *Oeuvres complètes. Textes et dernières paroles*,
                      Jacques Longchampt, ed. (Paris, 1992)
PN   *Poésies*
Pri   *Prières*
RP   *Récréations pieuses*

THE WORKS OF CHARLES PÉGUY

Beauce   *Présentation de la Beauce à Notre Dame de
                     Chartres*
Cinq prières   *Les cinq prières dans la cathédrale de Chartres*
Geneviève   *La tapisserie de Sainte Geneviève et de
                     Jeanne d'Arc*
Innocents   *Le mystère des saints innocents*
Laudet   *Un nouveau théologien, M. Fernand Laudet*
Mystère   *Le mystère de la charité de Jeanne d'Arc*
Porche   *Le porche du mystère de la deuxième vertu*

OPC   *Oeuvres poétiques complètes* (Paris, 1954)
OPR 1   *Oeuvres en prose*, vol. 1, 1898–1908 (Paris, 1959)
OPR 2   *Oeuvres en prose*, vol. 2, 1908–1914 (Paris, 1961)

THE WORKS OF GEORGES BERNANOS

Journal   *Journal d'un curé de campagne*
OR   *Oeuvres romanesques* (Paris, 1961)

MISCELLANEOUS

Autobiography The Autobiography of G. K. Chesterton (New York, 1936)

Balthasar,
  Schwestern   *Schwestern im Geist. Thérèse von Lisieux und Elisabeth von Dijon*, new edition (Einsiedeln, 1990)

CCSL   *Corpus christianorum: series latina* (Turnhout, 1953ff.)

Dejond   Thierry Dejond, *Charles Péguy. L'espérance d'un salut universel* (Namur, 1989)

Léthel,
  Connaître   François-Marie Léthel OCD, *Connaître l'amour du Christ qui surpasse toute connaissance. La théologie des saints* (Venasque, 1989)

Mackey   Aidan Mackey, ed., *The Collected Works of G. K. Chesterton*, vol. 10, Collected Poetry, Part 1 (San Francisco, 1994)

Prière   Albert Béguin, *La prière de Péguy* (Neuchâtel, 1942)

SC   *Sources chrétiennes* (Paris, 1940ff.)

Ward, *Return* Maisie Ward, *Return to Chesterton* (London and New York, 1952)

All Scriptural quotations are taken from the Douay-Rheims Bible.

Preface

> A voice in Rama was heard, lamentation and great mourning;
> Rachel bewailing her children and would not be comforted,
> because they are not.
>   (Matt. 2:18; cf. Jer. 31:15)

The sin of the century is the sin against the child. The tears of Rachel have become an ocean. In the richest and most powerful country on earth, child abuse has been called 'a national emergency'.[1] More children have been wilfully killed by adults during the last hundred years than in the whole preceding history of the human race. The fact is beyond doubt. The numbers can be checked in the annals of every nation on earth. Sixty years ago the neo-pagans of National Socialism were appointing bureaucrats to implement a programme of children's euthanasia.[2] In the last thirty years, hundreds of

---

[1] In 1990, the US Advisory Board on Child Abuse outlined the proportions of the emergency in its official report *Child Abuse and Neglect. Critical First Steps in Response to a National Emergency* (Washington, 1990). In 1989 there were 2.4 million abused children in the USA.

[2] 'On 18 August 1939, the Reich Committee introduced the compulsory registering of all "malformed" newborn children . . . In return for a payment of 2RMs per case, doctors and midwives were obliged to report instances of idiocy and Down's Syndrome; microcephaly; hydrocephaly; physical deformities such as the absence of a limb or late development of the head or spinal column; and forms of spinal paralysis' (Michael Burleigh, *Death and Deliverance. 'Euthanasia' in Germany, c. 1900–1945* [Cambridge, 1994], pp. 93–129). Three or four years later, 'the killing of children, adolescents, and young adults had become routine and systematic . . . As many as 6,000 children died, although many more were killed under the adult "euthanasia" programme' (ibid., p. 111).

1

millions of the unborn have been butchered in dark satanic mills from Adelaide to Zurich.[3] Pharaoh and Herod massacred the innocents in sudden nights of rage, but their successors slay the lambs in the calm light of the day with industrial efficiency. The death of a little one can be secured by a consultation of the Yellow Pages. Arguments for infanticide are set forth with academic *sang-froid* in journals and dissertations.[4] One author, while claiming not to 'condone' the evil, has presented child abuse as 'an evolutionary mechanism associated with population-resource balance'.[5] A crime whose depravity once robbed moralists of speech is now loquaciously promoted in parliaments. The small and weak are robbed of their freedom to live by the great and mighty insisting on their freedom to 'choose'. Throughout Western Europe and North America there are well-endowed societies for the prevention of cruelty to children, but better funded by far, backed by national governments and international agencies, are bodies for the prevention of children.[6] And in China, under a tyranny whose

[3] See the United Nations Department of Economic and Social Development, *Abortion Policies. A Global Review* (New York, 1992).

[4] Michael Tooley concludes his book *Abortion and Infanticide* as follows: 'If the line of thought pursued above is correct, neither abortion, nor infanticide, at least during the first few weeks after birth, is morally wrong' (Oxford, 1983), p. 419. Peter Singer of Monash University in Australia describes as 'speciesist' any distinctions between human persons and non-human animals. He maintains that 'killing, say, a chimpanzee is worse than the killing of a gravely defective human who is not a person' (cited in M. Burleigh, op. cit., pp. 297f.).

[5] David Bakan, *Slaughter of the Innocents* (San Francisco, 1971), p. 3.

[6] See R. Marshall and C. Donovan, *Blessed are the Barren. The Social Policy of Planned Parenthood* (San Francisco, 1991). The links between the eugenicists who fathered the Birth Control movement in the USA and the architects of the euthanasia programme in Nazi Germany are well documented. Foster Kennedy, a eugenicist and member of the Euthanasia Society of the USA, received an honorary doctorate from the Nazis. He resigned from the Euthanasia Society because they favoured only 'voluntary' euthanasia, while he urged systematic extermination of 'creatures born defective'. 'Kennedy continued to promote euthanasia in the United States, even after the mass killings of mentally handicapped people in Nazi Germany had been revealed to the American people' (Stefan Kühl, *The Nazi Connection. Eugenics, American Racism, and German National Socialism* (New York and Oxford, 1994), pp. 86f.). In the very year in which the Second World War ended, the Jewish convert to Catholicism David Goldstein pointed out these same links in *Suicide Bent. Sangerizing Mankind* (St Paul, 1945).

abominations rank with Hitler's and Stalin's, there is state coercion into contraception, compulsory abortion, and widespread infanticide.

Modern men and women seem to have declared war on their children. In societies dedicated to the pursuit of unrestrained sexual pleasure, the child has become an obstacle to be circumvented, even an enemy to be destroyed. The dominant contraceptive mentality is intrinsically contra-child, for the contracepting person wills a child not to be. The cult of homosexuality, too, is a practical hatred of the child, because it is the rejection of woman and therefore of the fruit of her womb, an ultimate compact with sterility and death.[7]

The sin against the child is the sin of this and every century, the sin of the world. From the beginning, the fallen angel, who is proud and will not obey his Creator, has struck out at the child, whose very being signifies humility and the receptivity required for entry to the Kingdom. The Serpent is a perpetual enemy of the Seed of the Woman (cf. Gen. 3:15); he wants to kill and devour her Child (cf. Apoc. 12:4) – the Divine Child and in Him every child. In the ancient world only the Hebrews consistently raised their voices against the slaughter of children. The old religion of Canaan worshipped animals and sacrificed children. In dark groves they offered up the innocent to Moloch. The very name of the Jewish Hell, 'Gehenna', refers to the vile valley of slaughter, just south of Jerusalem, where children were butchered and burnt to placate 'the idols of Canaan' (cf. Ps. 105:38; Jer. 19:3–6). King David was in no doubt: 'the gods of the Gentiles', those false deities who demand the blood of children, 'are devils' (Ps. 95:5).

The words of Hans Urs von Balthasar are hard to refute: 'Everywhere outside of Christianity the child is automatically sacrificed.'[8] Not every individual pagan is guilty of the hatred

---

[7] The great Christian humanist Lactantius says this of pederastic corruption of the young: 'What can be sacred to these men who supplied their lust with children of tender age and in need of protection, destroying and defiling them? So great is this crime, I cannot speak of it. All I can say is that these men are impious and parricides' (*Divinae institutiones* 6, 23; PL 6. 717A).

[8] *Das Ganze im Fragment. Aspekte der Geschichtstheologie*, new edition (Einsiedeln, 1990), p. 282.

of children, but most pagan cultures tolerate the murder of children: if not by cult, then through abortion and infanticide. Reverence for the child is the gift of Christianity, the gift of Jesus Christ, to the world. It is part of the newness that, according to the Church Fathers, the divine Word incarnate brought into human history. And as the modern world turns away from the Virgin and her Child, who makes all things new, so it falls into the old vice of killing its young. The Norwegian Catholic writer Sigrid Undset once wrote:

> Where [the Virgin Mother] is driven away, there Herod slinks on his way back and people are seduced by the Idumean's dreams of power and pleasure, of feasts in newly built palaces and blood in dark cellars, and in their hearts Herod's hatred for his own descendants and his fear of children awaken. And the old visions of the goddesses of material change, gods of birth and decay, rising and falling life, again spring up.[9]

The spiritual combat of this and every age is the battle of the Lamb of God and His Bride against the child-devouring Dragon. At the dawn of the twentieth century, to equip His Church with fresh light and strength for the struggle, God raised up a band of prophets who proclaimed anew the truth, goodness, and beauty of childhood, both the natural childhood of the sons of Adam and the supernatural childhood of the adopted sons of God. The princess among these prophets is a saint and doctor of the Church, St Thérèse of Lisieux. In her retinue are four men, her spiritual brothers, whose writings are an amplification and development of her Little Way. Only one of them is a 'theologian' in the formal sense: the priest Hans Urs von Balthasar. The other three are laymen, fighting for Christ in the battlefields of literature and journalism: Gilbert Keith Chesterton, Charles Péguy, and Georges Bernanos. Chesterton makes his appearance in each chapter of the book. This is only fitting. He had a special gift of understanding and appreciating the work of his fellow writers. As once in his own career, so now in this book, G.K. plays M.C. In each chapter he

---

[9] Sigrid Undset, 'A Christmas Meditation', in *Sigrid Undset on Saints and Sinners. New Translations and Studies* (San Francisco, 1993), p. 285.

offers a generous word of introduction and makes a grateful speech of conclusion.

Chesterton, St Thérèse, and the other members of our famous five were born between the Franco-Prussian War and the First World War. They are prophets of the end of the age. The study of their lives disturbs the complacent ideological readings of the conflicts of our century. There is only one *grande bataille*: the fight for the Christ Child against the Antichrists who deny Him and seek to destroy Him in the smallest of His brethren. There is only one way to victory and to peace: the way of the Lamb.

> These follow the Lamb whithersoever He goeth. These were purchased from among men, the firstfruits to God and to the Lamb. And in their mouth was found no lie.
>
> (Apoc. 14:4–5)

1

They Followed the Lamb

The Little Way of Thérèse Martin
and Gilbert Chesterton

St Thérèse of Lisieux and G. K. Chesterton were both children of the 1870s. Had Kensington been closer to Alençon, they might even have played together by the same pavilion in the park.[1] Thérèse is older than Gilbert by a year, though it is hard to think of her as anything but the youngest sister, and he will always seem the biggest of big brothers. By the Providence of God, these two heroes of the faith – the Little Flower of the Child Jesus and the Large Knight of the Holy Ghost – were born and spent their childhood in the same late Victorian age. I believe, and I hope here to show, that God gave them to the last century in its decline and to this century at its dawn for a similar mission and with a common message. Along different paths – by the vows of religion from Les Buissonnets to Carmel, by the vows of marriage from Grub Street to Beaconsfield – they followed the Lamb of God wherever He went (cf. Apoc. 14:4). Drawn by His star, they made a journey to Bethlehem, and as they knelt by the Manger, to the wise men of the world they said: 'Unless you convert and become like *this* Little Child, you will not enter the Kingdom of Heaven' (cf. Matt. 18:3).

Thérèse is a canonized saint and doctor of the Church. Officially, Chesterton is neither, though, in the minds of many, he is one of Christendom's wisest fathers and, in the hearts of a few,

---

[1] 'I remember with happiness the days when Papa took us to the *pavillon*. The smallest details are engraved on my heart' (MS A, 11v, OC 86).

one of its saintliest sons. In what follows, both will be my
teachers, but of the two, as is fitting, the canonized saint will
enjoy a primacy of attention and authority. Kindliest and most
chivalrous of men, Gilbert will gladly let his voice be the echo
of a maiden's, his song be harmony for the melody of a saint.

I. The Night of the Nineties

1. St Thérèse's Night of Faith

It is the summer of 1897, and Thérèse is following the Lamb
into the night. Since Good Friday of the previous year, her body
has been racked by disease, and her soul by temptations to
doubt. When the first symptom of consumption appeared, she
exulted in the hope of Heaven, but joy has been displaced by
anguish. She is tempted with the thought that the atheists are
right, that after death there is nothing.[2] She begs her sister
Pauline (in Carmel, Mother Agnès) for the protection of her
prayers:

> Pray for me, that I don't listen to the devil, who wants to convince
> me of so many lies. The thinking of the worst materialists is
> pressing down on my mind: the idea that eventually, as it goes on
> making new progress, science will explain everything naturally
> ... etc etc.[3]

When she sings of the happiness of Heaven, she feels no joy,
'because I am singing simply of what I want to believe'.[4] The
voice of darkness mocks her: 'Come on, come on, delight in
death. It won't give you what you hope for. All it will give you
is a still deeper night, the night of nothingness.'[5] On one black

---

[2] 'During those very happy days of Eastertide, Jesus made me feel that there
really are souls who have no faith, who through their misuse of grace lose this
precious treasure, the source of the only true and pure joy. He permitted my
soul to be engulfed by the thickest darkness and the thought of Heaven, once
so sweet to me, to be a subject of nothing but conflict and torment ... This trial
was not to last a few days, a few weeks; it was not to cease till the hour
determined by the good God, and ... that hour has still not come' (MS C, 5v,
OC 241).
[3] DE, August 1897, OC 1177.
[4] MS C, 7v, OC 244.
[5] MS C, 6v, OC 243.

day of pain, when the TB struck her kidneys, she confessed that 'if she had not had faith, she would not have hesitated for a moment to put herself to death'.[6]

Thérèse is not losing her faith but using it, wielding it as a buckler in the battle against mankind's ancestral foe.[7] 'I think I have made more acts of faith this past year than during the whole of my life.'[8] In faith, she offers up the torment of temptation against faith for those who have no faith at all:

> I offer these very great pains to obtain the light of faith for poor unbelievers, for all who remove themselves from the beliefs of the Church.[9]

For the love of Christ, she reaches out to the faithless and prays in her own and their name: 'Have pity on us, Lord, for we are poor sinners' (cf. Luke 18:13).[10]

Thérèse's trial of faith is not the Dark Night described by her master, St John of the Cross.[11] His nights of sense and spirit are

---

[6] Note from the *Cahiers verts* (CJ, 22 August 1897, OC 1104). Cf. CJ, 23 September 1897, OC 1133. According to Mother Agnès, the temptations against faith intensified as death approached on 30 September 1897. Thérèse asked for her bed to be sprinkled with holy water. Mother Agnès went to pray before the statue of the Sacred Heart: 'O Sacred Heart, I beg you, grant that my little sister does not die in despair' (cf. Father Marie-Eugène OCD, *Ton amour a grandi avec moi. Un génie spirituel – Thérèse de Lisieux* [Venasque, 1987], p. 78).

[7] With reference to St Thérèse, one of the great spiritual masters of this century, the Servant of God Father Marie-Eugène OCD, once wrote: 'Temptation against faith can be suffered by souls with a high degree of faith, to supply that redemptive suffering that merits for others light to walk in the way of salvation ... The description given by St Thérèse of the Child Jesus shows us a temptation coming from darkness and obsession, whose violence calls forth a more and more firm and tenacious assent to truth, and discloses the redemptive character of such a trial. The perfection of the virtue of faith ... is not measured by the peace that accompanies it. A very strong and pure faith can know great torments' (*I Want to See God. A Practical Synthesis of Carmelite Spirituality*, vol. 1 [Notre Dame, 1953], p. 543).

[8] MS C 7r, OC 243.

[9] DE, to Mother Agnès, August 1897, OC 1178.

[10] MS C, 6r, OC 242.

[11] 'Thérèse's trial is not ... the simple trial of faith that stems from the essential obscurity of faith, the trial of which St John of the Cross speaks, especially in Book II of *The Ascent of Mount Carmel*. Moreover, Thérèse uses the very significant phrase "trial against faith"' (Léthel, *Connaître*, pp. 522f.).

a purgation for the sake of union, a preparation for mystical marriage with Christ. But Thérèse is already in the unitive way; the wedding bond is sealed.[12] 'O Jesus, my divine Spouse,' she prays at her Profession, 'let me seek or find nought but you.'[13] Her present darkness is a mystery *within* the marriage. The Bridegroom is giving His young Bride a dowry at once tender and terrible: co-operation with Him in the saving of souls through participation in His own abandonment on the Cross.[14] The Triune God is taking up Thérèse's offer to be a 'holocaust victim to His merciful love'.[15]

On Calvary, the Son of God took on, in order to take away, the monstrous burden of the sins of the world. The sinless Saviour became sin so that the unrighteous might become the righteousness of God (cf. 2 Cor. 5:21). Now He asks Thérèse to share in that 'wonderful exchange'.[16] He calls her to enter the strange *chiaroscuro* of His Passion, that coincidence of delight and dereliction of which the Schoolmen speak. According to St Thomas Aquinas, the soul of the suffering Jesus, while resting at its summit in the blissful vision of the Father, was at the same time plunged into a grief beyond measure, the feeling of being

[12] I am indebted to the work of my colleague, Father Frederick L. Miller, for this interpretation of St Thérèse. He expounds it in *The Trial of Faith of St Thérèse of Lisieux* (Staten Island, 1998). With regard to the compatibility of the state of transforming union with the trial of faith, Father Miller argues as follows: '[T]rials are by no means incompatible with the state of mystical marriage and, in fact, provide an opportunity for the soul in that state to participate more deeply in Christ's sacrifice for the salvation of the world' (p. 189).

[13] Pri 2, 'Billet de Profession', 8 September 1890, OC 957. See Miller, op. cit., pp. 173ff.

[14] In the *Carnet jaune*, Thérèse says: 'Our Lord died on the Cross in anguish, and yet that is the most beautiful death of love … To die of love is not to die in ecstasy. I tell you frankly, I think that's what I am experiencing' (4 July 1897, OC 1023).

[15] Cf. Pri 6, OC 962.

[16] 'She lives the wonderful and terrible exchange which takes place between the merciful love of Jesus penetrating the heart of the sinner to give him life and the sin of man penetrating the Heart of Jesus to give Him suffering and death' (Léthel, p. 421). On the Fathers' understanding of the 'wonderful exchange' (*admirabile commercium*) effected by the Incarnation and saving work of the Son of God, see Hans Urs von Balthasar, *Theodramatik*, vol. 3, Die Handlung (Einsiedeln, 1980), pp. 226ff.

forsaken by the Father.[17] Chesterton alludes to this mystery in
Orthodoxy: in the Heart of the God-Man there was a 'gigantic
secret' of joy, and yet, in His dereliction on the Cross, 'God
seemed for an instant to be an atheist'.[18] In substitution for
sinners, the spotless Lamb tasted and overcame, as Pope John
Paul has written, 'the suffering which is separation, rejection
by the Father, estrangement from God'.[19] Similarly, Thérèse, in
union with the Beloved, without losing her faith in Him, is
allowed to experience the desolation of the faithless, not just
of innocent unbelievers, but of unrepentant infidels, in order
to win them the grace of conversion. She is suffering not
because of her own sins – she knows that she has never committed a mortal sin – but because of the sins of her brethren.[20]
Her very innocence is a force of connection, for sin separates
even sinners from each other; holiness alone can unite.[21] In

[17] Cf. St Thomas Aquinas, *Summa theologiae* 3a 46, 7 & 8. St Thomas says that
Christ enjoyed the Beatific Vision in His 'higher reason', while He suffered in
all His soul's other powers. However, since the powers of the soul are rooted
in its essence, the whole soul knew both joy and sorrow, though not in the
same powers. St Thérèse believed that she had been given the grace to
experience something of the coincidence of joy and sorrow in the soul of the
suffering Christ. On 6 July 1897 she told Mother Agnès that she had discovered
a beautiful passage in the *Imitation*: 'In the Garden of Gethsemane, Our Lord
enjoyed all the delights of the Trinity, and yet His agony was no less cruel.
This is a mystery, but I assure you that I understand something of it, because I
experience it myself' (CJ, OC 1025). See my book *The Mysteries of March. Hans
Urs von Balthasar on the Incarnation and Easter* (London, 1990), pp. 55f.

[18] *The Collected Works of G. K. Chesterton*, vol. 2 (San Francisco, 1986), pp. 343,
365f.

[19] Cf. *Salvifici doloris*, n. 18.

[20] 'While the soul described by St John of the Cross suffers because of its
own sins, the deep roots of its sins, its own darkness, Thérèse suffers because
of the sins, the darkness, of others' (Léthel, p. 523). Just after her entry into
Carmel, she made a general confession and was told by the priest at the time:
'In the presence of the Good God, the Blessed Virgin, and all the saints, I declare
that you have never committed a single mortal sin' (MS A, 70r, OC 187).

[21] 'It is paradoxically the extreme innocence of Thérèse which makes her
close to sinners ... [W]ithout any sin against faith, Thérèse becomes, for the
faithless, sin against faith, so that the faithless may become the justice of God'
(Léthel, *Connaître*, pp. 517, 519). One must not rigidify the contrast between
purgation of one's own sins and reparation for those of others. As Father Léthel
goes on to say, 'the personal purification described by St John of the Cross has
a redemptive dimension: the triumph of love in one soul has an effect on the

her darkness, Thérèse prays for light for the unbelieving and makes reparation for their blasphemies: 'May all those who are not enlightened by the bright torch of faith at last come to see it shine.'[22]

Thérèse's 'night of faith', in imitation of Mary's at the foot of the Cross, is co-redemptive.[23] Just as the Mother of God by her night of faith co-operated with the objective redemption, the meriting of grace by her crucified Son, so the Little Flower by her night of faith co-operates with the subjective redemption, the communication of grace by the glorified Son. Her heart goes out to the godless, to bring them the gift of conversion. She even offers up her last Holy Communion for the apostate Carmelite priest, Hyacinthe Loyson.[24] At the heart of the Church, she is fulfilling an apostolate of love, a bold mission *in partibus infidelium*.

2. Chesterton's Night

The darkness that envelops young Thérèse is the night of the Nineties. It seemed to some a very black night indeed.[25] Chesterton describes it in the poem he wrote as a dedication to his boyhood friend E. C. Bentley for his novel *The Man Who Was Thursday*:

---

whole Mystical Body. Likewise, at the heart of her redemptive suffering, Thérèse continues to need purification. Only Jesus and Mary were absolutely without sin, Jesus as Saviour, Mary as first of the saved' (ibid., p. 523).

[22] Ibid. 'Were my suffering really unknown to you (which is impossible), I'd still be happy to have it, if through it I was able to prevent or make reparation for a single offence committed against the faith' (MS C, 7r, OC 243).

[23] In her great Mariological poem, 'Why I love you, O Mary', Thérèse says: 'Mother, your sweet Child wants you to be the example / Of the soul that seeks Him in the *night of faith*' (PN 54, OC 753). In *Redemptoris mater*, Pope John Paul II speaks at length of Our Lady's 'kenosis of faith' on Calvary (cf. n. 18).

[24] See the *Cahiers verts* for 19 August 1897 (CJ, 20 August 1897, OC 1099n).

[25] Chesterton's friend Maurice Baring did not remember the decade as 'peculiar, exciting, and exotic', but then 'the process of change which is never ending was, as it always is, imperceptible to those who were partaking of it and living in it' ('The Nineties', in *Lost Lectures or the Fruits of Experience* [New York, 1932], p. 73).

A cloud was on the mind of men, and wailing went the weather,
Yea, a sick cloud upon the soul when we were boys together.
Science announced nonentity and art admired decay ...[26]

Chesterton confesses in his *Autobiography* that he took up writing as a protest against the negativity of the Nineties: 'I was full of a new and fiery resolution to write against the Decadents and the Pessimists who ruled the culture of the age.'[27] This was after he had been nearly swept away in the torrent of nothingness. By the age of sixteen he was a complete agnostic and at nineteen was dabbling in spiritualism and having close encounters with diabolists and decadents. His imagination had become a playground for the irrational. 'As Bunyan, in his morbid period, described himself as prompted to utter blasphemies, I had an overpowering impulse to record or draw horrible ideas and images; plunging deeper and deeper as in a blind spiritual suicide.'[28] He was saved, as we shall see, by childhood – by the memory of his own childhood, but even more by the childhood of the Virgin's Son.[29]

3. Scepticism, Pessimism, Egoism

Thérèse was in the cloister, but she had seen and felt the 'sick cloud' that hung above the world.[30] Carmel, for her as for all the daughters of St Teresa, was a heaven-haven but not a safe haven, the fighting fortress of the Queen of Carmel not a refuge from the world's woes. Thérèse was in the thick of the spiritual battle and vulnerable to all the darts and spears of the enemy. Five months before her death, on 19 April 1897, Leo Taxil revealed that his story of the conversion of the Satanist, Diana Vaughan, through the intercession of Joan of Arc, was a hoax, a

[26] Mackey, pp. 324f.
[27] *Autobiography*, p. 91.
[28] Ibid., pp. 92f.
[29] This salvation through childhood is beautifully described by Joseph Pearce in *Wisdom and Innocence. A Life of G. K. Chesterton* (San Francisco, 1996), pp. 27ff.
[30] 'The weight that Thérèse painfully bears in her Passion is the weight of sin against faith, at the root of the dechristianization of the old world, the passage from faith to unbelief' (Léthel, *Connaître*, p. 523).

joke at the expense of the Church. Like many other Catholics, including Pope Leo XIII himself, Thérèse had been hoodwinked; she had even sent Diana a photograph of herself, dressed as Joan of Arc, which Taxil projected onto a screen at his press conference. 'On 9 June, she wrote one of the most touching pages of her autobiography, mentioning those "impious people" who have lost their faith "through the abuse of graces". How could she not have in mind the hoaxer who had just thrown off his mask? She offers her trial for him.'[31]

The Taxil episode is proof that, if the Nineties were daringly naughty, it was only because, to be philosophically and etymologically more exact, they were deadeningly nihilistic. In both France and England, the culture seemed to be flooded by Scepticism, Pessimism, and Egoism, the brazen disavowal of faith, hope, and charity.

The Nineties were a decade of scepticism, of doubt and denial of God. 'Make no mistake about it', declared Nietzsche, 'great minds are sceptics ... Convictions are prisons.'[32] By the time Thérèse is suffering her trial of faith, Nietzsche has long been mad and will soon be dead, but in London his scepticism is ensnaring many intellectuals, including some of the later friends of Chesterton.[33] In Germany, Richard Strauss, who has just composed his Nietzschean tone poem *Also sprach Zarathustra*, is declaring that 'the German nation can gain new energy only through liberation from Christianity'.[34] In Siberia, the exiled Lenin shoots duck and plots the execution of Holy Russia.[35] In France, the apostate Renan, having seduced two generations

[31] A note by the editors in the Longchampt edition of St Thérèse's works (OC 1433).

[32] *Der Antichrist*, n. 54; *Friedrich Nietzsche Werke*, vol. 2, K. Schlechta, ed. (Munich, 1966), p. 1220.

[33] See Patrick Bridgwater, *Nietzsche in Anglosaxony. A Study of Nietzsche's Impact on English and American literature* (Leicester, 1972), pp. 11ff. and passim. The chief Nietzschean among Chesterton's friends was, of course, George Bernard Shaw, who provided the English-speaking world with the translation of *Übermensch* – 'Superman' (the earlier version was 'Overman').

[34] Gustav Mahler – Richard Strauss, *Briefwechsel 1888–1911*, H. Blaukopf, ed. (Munich, 1988), p. 211.

[35] See Robert Service, *Lenin. A Political Life*, vol. 1 (Bloomington, 1985), pp. 63f.

with his scented prose, is in his grave but still remembered and widely mourned as a hero of the Republic. For over ten years, the Abbé Loisy, high priest of Modernism, has not accepted literally a single article of the Creed except for 'crucified under Pontius Pilate'.[36]

As Chesterton observes somewhere, when men lose their faith in God, they end up believing, not in nothing, but in anything. There is none so credulous as the sceptic. Man, created in God's image, is religious by nature, and so, when in the folly of his heart he says that there is no God, his inclination to worship finds other objects. As the Apostle says, they exchange the truth of God for a lie and serve the creature rather than the Creator (cf. Rom. 1:25). The unbelievers of the Nineties all had shrines at which they worshipped. Renan, for example, made himself the votary of Science.[37] Many others wandered off into Spiritualism and the Occult.

The Nineties were a decade of pessimism. With the loss of faith came the abandonment of hope. In the Germany of this period, there is – to use Balthasar's phrase – a widespread 'deification of death' (*Vergöttlichung des Todes*), which will swiftly become the sacralizing of suicide.[38] Nietzsche's Zarathustra commends 'the free death that comes to me because *I* will it'.[39] Rilke, already at work on his first poems, glorifies the 'Great Death', the death that *I* die with full autonomy, as opposed to the 'petty death' that 'they' die.[40] Such pessimism in the individual is the inexorable consequence of the cult of Progress for the race. During the

---

[36] Alfred Loisy, *My Duel with the Vatican. The Autobiography of a Catholic Modernist* (ET New York, 1924), p. 128. See Marvin R. O'Connell, *Critics on Trial. An Introduction to the Catholic Modernist Crisis* (Washington, 1994), passim.

[37] In his *Lettre à M. Marcellin Berthelot*, he says that 'the final resurrection will take place through science' (*Oeuvres complètes de Ernest Renan*, vol. 1 [Paris, 1947], p. 650). See the texts from *L'Avenir de la science* quoted with loathing by Péguy in 'Zangwill' (p. 66 below).

[38] This is the title of the third volume of his *Apokalypse der deutschen Seele* (Salzburg, 1939). Based on his doctoral dissertation, it concludes Balthasar's analytic history of modern German literature and philosophy. It studies, among others, Scheler, Heidegger, Rilke, Barth, and Bloch.

[39] 'Vom freien Tode', *Also sprach Zarathustra, Friedrich Nietzsche Werke*, vol. 2, K. Schlechta, ed. (Munich, 1966), p. 334.

[40] Rainer Maria Rilke, 'Das Stunden-Buch', *Sämtliche Werke*. Werkausgabe, vol. 1 (Frankfurt, 1976), p. 347.

Nineties, the liberating Last Things of Christianity were being discarded for the fatalistic finalities of atheism: Scientific Advance, the Evolution of Superman, the Communist Revolution. Everything was suddenly and self-consciously 'new'.[41] Joachim of Fiore's prophecies of a coming 'third age' of spiritual liberty live on in new and ever darker forms.[42] This expectation of a 'new age' was but an eagerness born of despair. It was a hope, not in God, nor for the glorious coming of our Saviour Jesus Christ, but for the final outcome of a mechanistic and godless process. The Victorian Materialists would not say in faith, 'I know that my Redeemer liveth', and so they could not add in hope, 'and in the last day I shall rise out of the earth' (Job 19:25). By contrast, the Spiritualists might aspire to an after-life of spectral survival, but they lacked the full-bodied, theocentric confidence of Job: 'In my flesh I shall see my God' (v. 26).

The Nineties were a decade of Egoism. Charity, self-giving, was being displaced by a new fashion of self-worship. For Nietzsche, compassion was a humiliation.[43] The good was whatever 'heightens in man the sense of power, the will to power'.[44] The Great Man, the Superman, would answer to no one but himself, in Alpine isolation above all fellow feeling. In 1898 a British journal, *The Eagle and the Serpent*, was founded to promote Nietzsche's 'egoistic philosophy' under the slogan, 'A Race of Freemen is necessarily a Race of Egoists'.[45] In the lavender salons of the 'Decadents', such egoism became the narcissism of unnatural vice. Pessimism and Perversity minced through the Nineties hand in hand. During the Spring of Thérèse's final

[41] See Holbrook Jackson's classic study, *The Eighteen Nineties. A Review of Art and Ideas at the Close of the Nineteenth Century* (New York, 1922), passim.

[42] The thousand-year 'Third Reich' of Nazi neo-paganism is a later example of this 'spiritual posterity' (cf. H. de Lubac, *La postérité spirituelle de Joachim de Flore*, vol. 2, De Saint-Simon à nos jours [Paris, 1981], pp. 382f.).

[43] 'They call Christianity the religion of *compassion (Midleids)*. Compassion is the antithesis of the tonic affections that heighten the energy of the sense of life: compassion has a depressive effect ... Compassion in general cuts across the law of development, which is the law of *selection' (Der Antichrist*, n. 7; *Friedrich Nietzsche Werke*, vol. 2, K. Schlechta, ed. (Munich, 1966), p. 1168).

[44] Ibid., n. 2, p. 1165.

[45] See Holbrook Jackson, *The Eighteen Nineties*, p. 129.

agony, Oscar Wilde was released from Reading Gaol, chastened but not yet chaste.

4. The Onslaught on Childhood

The attack on Christianity during the Eighteen Nineties was also, was above all, an onslaught on *childhood*. The Antichrist philosophies were all radically anti-child, disdainful of the spirit of the child and ultimately destructive of his life. The late Victorians looked back with pride at Lord Shaftesbury's rescue of children from chimneys and mines, and yet in their own very comfortable era a still more horrible oppression was being planned for the young.

In Balthasar's words already quoted, 'everywhere outside of Christianity the child is automatically sacrificed'.[46] The movement away from Christ is always a turn towards Moloch, the god who demands the blood of children. Pagan antiquity saw the child as an 'imperfect, half-finished human being',[47] 'a preliminary stage before full humanness',[48] and therefore an object to be used or discarded at will. At the end of the second century Tertullian notes that infanticide was widespread among the pagans.[49] The *Didache*, which dates from the first century, contrasts the Christian 'Way of Life', where men love God and neighbour and do not 'corrupt boys' and murder children by abortion or after birth, with the 'Way of Death' of the pagans, who are 'murderers of children' and 'corrupters of God's creation'.[50] It shocks the Christian reader of Plato and Aristotle to find, alongside so much that is true and good, the recommendation that 'defective offspring' be disposed of.[51] Plato saw the child as an inferior being, to be classed with slaves, women, and beasts,[52] while Aristotle supported the state's right to fix a

[46] *Das Ganze im Fragment*, p. 282.
[47] Ibid.
[48] Cf. Hans Urs von Balthasar, *Wenn ihr nicht werdet wie dieses Kind* (Ostfidern, 1988), p. 9.
[49] Cf. *Ad nationes* 1, 15; PL 1.580AB.
[50] *Didachê tôn apostolôn*, nn. 2 & 5; J. B. Lightfoot, ed., *The Apostolic Fathers*, revised edition (London, 1907), pp. 218, 220.
[51] Cf. Plato, *Republic*, 460C, 461BC; Aristotle, *Politics* 1335B.
[52] Cf. *Republic* 431C; *Theaetetus* 171E.

limit on the size of families and recommended early abortion ('before sense and life have begun') whenever a child was conceived beyond the authorized number.[53] Later, among the dualistic cults of Gnosticism and Manichaeanism, conceiving a child became a graver sin than fornication: debauchery displayed an 'enlightened' contempt for the body, but conception entangled a hapless soul in the flesh.[54]

Chesterton once spoke of paganism's 'mystical hatred of the idea of childhood' and suggested that 'people would understand better the popular fury against the witches, if they remembered that the malice most commonly attributed to them was preventing the birth of children. The Hebrew prophets were perpetually protesting against the Hebrew race relapsing into an idolatry that involved such a war upon children'.[55] The New Testament name for Hell, 'Gehenna', derives from the name of a place south of Jerusalem, 'the valley of the sons of Hinnom', where from the reign of King Ahaz to that of Manasseh, thousands of children were burnt in sacrifice to Moloch 'according to the abominable practices of the nations whom the Lord drove out before the people of Israel' (2 Kings 16:3). God's wrath is enkindled, says Jeremiah, because 'they have built the high places of Topheth, which is in the valley of the son of Hinnom, to burn their sons and daughters in the fire' (Jer. 7:31). With a divinely inspired incandescence of rage, King David denounces the apostate Israelites who sacrificed the blood of their children to 'the idols of Canaan' (cf. Ps. 105:38). Fidelity to the God of the covenant meant life for Israel's children. Infidelity was their sentence of death.

[53] Cf. *Politics* 1335B. See John M. Riddle, *Contraception and Abortion from the Ancient World to the Renaissance* (Cambridge and London, 1992), passim.

[54] According to St Irenaeus, the Gnostic leaders Saturninus and Basilides despised the body so much that the satisfying of any lusts was a matter of indifference, but marriage and the bearing of children were 'from Satan' (cf. *Adversus haereses* 1, 24, 3; PG 7. 675A). Addressing Faustus the Manichee, St Augustine says: 'You are taught by a devilish doctrine to regard your parents as enemies, because their union brought you into the bonds of the flesh' (*Contra Faustum Manichaeum* 15, 7; PL 42. 310). What the Manichees hated most about marriage was the procreation of children.

[55] *The Everlasting Man*, in *The Collected Works of G. K. Chesterton*, vol. 2, p. 254.

The New Paganism of the Nineties continued the campaign
of the Old against childhood, this time with the fury of a
conscious repudiation of Christianity. In a post-Darwinian age
enfatuated with Evolution and Progress, 'young' became a
synonym of 'undeveloped' and 'incomplete', and childhood was
seen as a stage to be left behind on the journey towards authentic
humanity. The weakness of Everyman's childhood was an
embarrassment to those who glorified the willpower of Superman's adulthood. Nietzsche dismissed Our Lord's welcoming
of the little ones as mere 'sentimentality'.[56] According to Karl
Marx, childhood is a state of dependence and therefore a synonym of slavery, the feudal era in the history of the individual.
Only when a human being is independent, indebted to no one,
does he truly become a person. Belief in the Creator is to be
rejected because it maintains all mankind in the servile, infantile
posture of dependence.[57] Nietzsche agreed: being a child for
life sounds nice, but in reality it means being a serving lad for
life.[58] It is the old Greek contempt: *pais* as both slave and child.

[56] 'The happiness of a child is as much of a myth as the happiness of the
Hyperboreans of Greek fable. The Greeks thought that, *if* happiness dwells
anywhere at all on earth, it must certainly dwell as far as possible from us,
perhaps over there, at the edge of the world. Old people have the same thought:
if man is at all capable of being happy, he must be happy as far as possible
from our age, at the frontiers and beginnings of life. For many a person, the
sight of children, through the veil of this myth, is the greatest happiness he
can experience. He enters into the forecourt of Heaven when he says, "Suffer
the little children to come unto me, for of them is the Kingdom of Heaven".
The myth of the child's Kingdom of Heaven holds good, in some way or other,
wherever in the modern world some sentimentality exists' (*Menschliches,
Allzumenschliches*, Zweiter Band, Der Wanderer und Sein Schatten, n. 265,
Friedrich Nietzsche Werke, vol. 1, K. Schlechta [Munich, 1966], p. 977).
[57] 'A being regards itself as independent only when it stands on its feet; and
it stands on its own feet only when it owes its existence to itself alone. A man
who lives by the grace of another considers himself a dependent being. But I
live by the grace of another completely if I owe him not only the maintenance
of my life but also its creation, if he is the source of my life; and my life
necessarily has such a cause outside itself if it is not my own creation'
(*Frühschriften*, S. Landshut, ed. [Stuttgart, 1953], p. 246). On Marx's view of the
child, see F. Ulrich, *Der Mensch als Anfang. Zur philosophischen Anthropologie der
Kindheit* (Einsiedeln, 1970), pp. 11ff.
[58] *Menschliches, Allzumenschliches*, Zweiter Band, Vermischte Meinungen und
Sprüche, n. 244, *Friedrich Nietzsche Werke*, vol. 1, K. Schlechta, ed. (Munich,
1966), p. 832.

When the child does emerge as a positive symbol in Nietzsche's writings, he is a monster: he is a 'new beginning', but he has neither father nor mother. He is just 'a game, a self-moving wheel, a first movement, a holy affirmation'.[59] The Nietzschean child is everything a real child is not, a metaphor of truculent autonomy and self-assertion.

But did the despiser of childhood not remember that he was once helpless in his mother's womb and at her breast, that he once skipped and laughed and played? How could this reality of human life be forgotten or ignored? Consigning the obvious to oblivion is the tell-tale trick of Gnosticism in both its ancient and modern forms. As Eric Voegelin has shown, the Gnosticism of Marx requires the suppression of man's first and most fundamental questions:

> Man knows himself as a link in the chain of being, and of necessity he will ask: where is the chain suspended? And can we answer the inopportune questioner? Marx gives the same answer as Comte: don't ask such questions; they are 'abstractions'; they make 'no sense' ...[60]

Marx must at all costs snuff out the child's wonder, the childlike man's wonder, for 'I wonder why' will lead to 'I wonder why there is something rather than nothing', the question whose answer is God.

The anti-child Prometheanism of the Nineties asserted itself within religion in the form of Liberal Protestantism and Modernism. The Modernists were openly in rebellion against the faith of their childhood and its wonder.[61] As the childlike Pope St Pius X perceived, the Modernists wanted a Christianity re-cast to the requirements of 'Modern Man' and his upward evolution, a more 'grown-up' religion.[62] 'At the present hour',

---

[59] *Also sprach Zarathustra* I, *Friedrich Nietzsche Werke*, vol. 2, p. 294.

[60] Eric Voegelin, in John H. Hallowell, ed. *From Enlightenment to Revolution* (Durham, 1975), p. 290. Cf. the same author's *Science, Politics, and Gnosticism* (Chicago, 1968), pp. 27ff.

[61] 'I never regained the simple faith of my childhood' (Alfred Loisy, *My Duel with the Vatica*, p. 168).

[62] 'To the laws of evolution,' said St Pius, 'everything is subject—dogma, Church, worship, the Books we revere as sacred, even faith itself' (*Pascendi dominici gregis* [1907], n. 26).

complained Loisy, 'the Church is an obstacle to the intellectual development of humanity.'[63] The Modernist Nineties were years of superior disdain for childlike orthodoxy, as Paul Claudel recalls:

> I take myself back again in thought to that sinister period, 1890 to 1910, in which my youth and maturity were spent, a period of aggressive and triumphant materialism and scepticism, dominated by the figure of Ernest Renan. What efforts were then made to obscure the divinity of Christ, to veil that unbearable Face, to flatten the Christian fact, to efface its contours beneath bandages of erudition and doubt.[64]

Religious liberalism was not just hostile to the child in its metaphors ('Adult Faith', 'Christianity Come of Age', and so on). The first thrust of its strategy was an assault on the mystery of Christmas, on the Child-God and His Virgin Mother.[65] It was in the Nihilistic Nineties, in 1892 in fact, that Adolf von Harnack and twenty-four other Liberal Protestant Prussians published the 'Declaration of Eisenach', which stated that no 'decisive significance for faith' could be attached to 'the narratives found in the opening chapters of the first and third Gospels'.[66] Lutherans no longer needed to believe in the historicity of the Infancy Gospels. This robbed human childhood of its highest glory, its assumption by the Son of God.

The attack on childhood during the Nineties is more than just a theory. The new Herods have practical ambitions. Evolutionism is itself evolving into Eugenics. Charles Darwin's cousin, Francis Galton, is drawing the blueprint for a Eugenics Education Society, finally established in 1907. In England and Germany, the 'intellectuals' are talking about the selective

[63] *Mémoires pour servir à l'histoire religieuse de notre temps*, vol. 1, 1857–1900 (Paris, 1930), p. 119.

[64] Paul Claudel, *Oeuvres complètes*, vol. 28 (Paris, 1978), pp. 291f.

[65] Already in 1885 Loisy was denying that Isaiah 7:14 was a prophecy of the Virgin Birth of Christ (*Mémoires pour servir à l'histoire religieuse de notre temps*, vol. 1, p. 139).

[66] A. Harnack *et al.*, *Christliche Welt* 6 (1892), 949. See J. de Freitas Ferreira, *Conceiçao virginal de Jesus. Análise critica da pesquisa liberal protestante, desde a 'Declaraçao de Eisenach' até hoje, sobre o testemunho de Mt 1:18–25 e Lc 1:26–38* (Rome, 1980), passim.

breeding of the human race, and from Nietzsche to Hitler, there is an obsession with overpopulation.[67] The babies of the lower classes and races must be prevented from being born. The 'masses' are a mess to be wiped up and out. H. G. Wells spits out his hatred for 'these gall-stones of vicious, helpless, and pauper masses', and insists that the 'swarms of black, and brown, and dirty-white, and yellow people, who do not come into the new needs of efficiency', will 'have to go'.[68] In his *Modern Utopia* babies born with deformity or disease are killed, and adults who are morally or physically deficient are barred from reproducing.[69]

In 1897 the Birth Control movement in France is well advanced. Ever since the Enlightenment French rationalists such as Condorcet have been urging artificial means of population control. By 1830 the birth rate had dropped below thirty per thousand.[70] The first contraceptive 'clinic' was opened in France in 1880.[71] In England it is twenty years since the atheist Charles Bradlaugh and the Theosophist Annie Besant won their appeal against conviction for distributing a pamphlet on 'family limitation'.[72] In France and England, married couples are beginning to regard the birth of a child not as a blessing to be treasured, but as a problem to be prevented, an obstacle to be circumvented. The openness to life of Thérèse's parents is rare and counter-cultural.[73]

The night of the Nineties was haunted by the shade of Herod. It is a striking fact that all three of the great Christian witnesses

[67] See John Carey, *The Intellectuals and the Masses. Pride and Prejudice among the Literary Intelligentsia, 1880–1939* (London, 1992), passim.

[68] *Anticipations of the Reaction of Mechanical and Scientific Progress upon Human Life and Thought* (New York, 1902), pp. 87 and 342.

[69] *A Modern Utopia* (London, 1905), p. 100. Some pages later Wells says that 'the ideal of a scientific civilization is to prevent those weaklings being born' (p. 126).

[70] See Angus McLaren, *A History of Contraception. From Antiquity to the Present Day* (Oxford, 1990), pp. 181f.

[71] See B. E. Finch and H. Green, *Contraception through the Ages* (Springfield, 1963), pp. 124ff.

[72] Ibid.

[73] See Sandra Misael, 'St Thérèse's Counter-cultural Family', *Catholic Twin Circle* (5–11 October 1997), 16.

who reached their majority during this decade (St Thérèse of Lisieux, G. K. Chesterton, and Charles Péguy) had a mysteriously intense devotion to the Holy Innocents, the babies slain by Herod in Bethlehem. Thérèse wrote a play on 'The Flight into Egypt'[74] and meditated often and at length on the unmerited Heaven of the Innocents.[75] Chesterton comes back to the theme time and again, perhaps most powerfully in the poem 'The Neglected Child', where he describes how 'naked / And monstrous and obscene / A tyrant bathed in all the blood / Of men that might have been.'[76] Later, only two years before the Great War, Charles Péguy, who was born in the same month as St Thérèse, wrote his epic poem on the *Mystère des saints innocents*, those 'simple children [who] play with their palm and martyrs' crowns'.[77] These three prophets, this 'daughter of Elijah'[78] and her two brothers, perceived that modernity's attempt to suppress Christ would end with a new slaughter of the innocents. They saw that the Dragon was desperate to devour the Child of the Woman and, in Him, every child (cf. Apoc. 12:4),[79] for the child is humility, the model of Christian discipleship, and the Dragon, the Devil, is pride,[80] the implacable foe of every true follower of Christ. I hope to show in the rest of this chapter

---

[74] The angels sing in chorus: 'Ineffable mystery / Jesus, the King of Heaven / Exiled on Earth / Flees before a mortal' ('La fuite en Egypte', RP 6, OC 891).

[75] See p. 31 above.

[76] 'The Neglected Child', Mackey, p. 84.

[77] OPC, p. 461. See pp. 94ff. below.

[78] 'True daughter of Elijah [founder of the Carmelite Order] that she is, the holy Carmelite of Lisieux has a complete prophetic mission' (Father Marie-Eugène, *Ton amour a grandi avec moi. Un génie spirituel: Thérèse de Lisieux* [Venasque, 1987], p. 100).

[79] In his encyclical *Evangelium vitae*, Pope John Paul II says: 'The Dragon wishes to devour "the child brought forth" (cf. Apoc. 12:4), a figure of Christ, whom Mary brought forth "in the fulness of time" (Gal. 4:4) and whom the Church must unceasingly offer to people in every age. *But in a way that child is also a figure of every person, every child, especially every helpless baby whose life is threatened, because, as the Council reminds us, "by His Incarnation the Son of God has united Himself in some fashion with every man"'* (n. 104 my italics).

[80] In his commentary on the Apocalypse, Richard of St Victor says that the Devil is 'a dragon in his cunning, huge in his pride (*elationem*), red by his cruelty' (*In Apocalypsim Ioannis* lib. 4; PL 196. 799C).

how St Thérèse and Chesterton took up arms in defence of holy
and lowly childhood.

II. The Lamp of the Lamb

And the city hath no need of the sun, nor of the moon, to shine in
it. For the glory of God hath enlightened it; and the Lamb is the
lamp thereof.
(Apoc. 21:23)

The Lamb is the lamp of the heavenly city, and through the
lives and writings of St Thérèse and Gilbert Chesterton, His light
has shone into our century. It is a light cast upon childhood, a
beam from the Burning Babe that falls upon every little member
of the family of man. The great doctrine of St Thérèse, which
Chesterton endorses, is the 'Little Way' of spiritual childhood.[81]

> So I can enjoy in Heaven your sweet presence
> I will practise all the virtues of childhood
> Did you not often say:
> 'Heaven is for the child'?[82]

In their own natural childhood, as in their teaching on spiritual
childhood, Thérèse and Gilbert refute the Herodianism of the
Nineties. Childhood is not a dull path to the bold highway of
adulthood, but rather, as Chesterton said, 'the white and solid
road and the worthy beginning of the life of man'.[83]

1. Confidence in the Father

The Little Way – Devotion to God the Father
The Little Way is first of all a devotion to God the Father, the
heavenly Father revealed by the only-begotten Son made man.
'Neither doth anyone know the Father but the Son and he to
whom it shall please the Son to reveal Him' (Matt. 11:27).

---

[81] St Thérèse's detailed exposition of the Little Way belongs to the last three
years of her life, after her sister Céline's entry into Carmel in September 1894.
The first allusion to it is in her letter to Céline of 23 July 1893 (cf. LT 144, OC
467ff.). Thérèse shares it with the novices and with her spiritual brother,
Seminarian Bellière.
[82] PN 24, OC 694.
[83] *Autobiography*, p. 49.

Through St Thérèse, it pleased the Son, in the Holy Spirit, not to add to the revelation He had already made of the Father, but to lead the Church to a more profound understanding of that revelation. The mission of the Little Flower is to sing of the unbounded compassion of God the Father,[84] to be a victim of His merciful love.[85]

> My Heaven is to remain for ever in His presence,
> To call Him my Father and to be His child.
> In His divine arms, I do not fear the storm.
> Total abandonment, that alone is my law.[86]

Jesus, the true and natural Son of God, called the Father 'Abba', a name of sweet endearment. Thérèse, daughter of God by the grace of her Baptism, *filia in Filio*, called the Father 'Papa'. Three months before her death, she said to Mother Agnès: 'Don't worry if you find me dead one morning. It'll just be because *Papa the Good God* has come to look for me.'[87] By the Providence of God, says Balthasar, 'Thérèse is born into a family which serves her, immediately and for ever, as an image of Heaven'.[88] Her *Papa* is an icon of the good God, and *Maman* is a type of Our Lady. Newly arrived in Carmel, she tells M. Martin in a letter: 'When I think of you, my dearest little Father, I naturally think of the good God, for it seems to me to be impossible to see anyone on earth holier than you.'[89] Catholics speak of the family as the 'Domestic Church', the presence in the home of the Church Militant on earth.[90] Thérèse, with exquisite theological accuracy,

---

[84] 'O my God, you have surpassed all my expectation, and as for me, I will sing of your mercies' (MS C, 3r, OC 238).

[85] MS A, 83v, OC 211f. As Father Conrad de Meester has said, faith in God's mercy is the foundation of the Little Way (see *Dynamique de la confiance. Genèse et structure de la voie d'enfance chez Ste Thérèse de Lisieux* [Paris, 1969], pp. 271f.).

[86] 'Mon Ciel à Moi!', PN 32, OC 715.

[87] CJ, 5 June 1897, OC 1009.

[88] Balthasar, *Schwestern*, p. 112.

[89] LT 58, to M. Martin, 31 July 1888, OC 352. One of the most touching tributes Thérèse pays to her father is his determination to preserve the innocence of his children. In a poem she says: 'O Papa, remember that in the days of her childhood / It was for God alone that you wanted to guard her innocence!' ('Prière de l'Enfant d'un Saint', PN 8, OC 651).

[90] Cf. the teaching of the Second Vatican Council, *Lumen gentium*, n. 11.

goes on to draw the conclusion that the family must also be a representation of the Church Triumphant in Heaven.

As the years went by, Thérèse came to see her father more as an icon of God the Son in His Passion than of God the Father in His Heaven.[91] When she was about seven, she had a vision of a man in the garden, dressed like her father but with his head veiled.[92] She eventually realized that this was a prophecy of Louis Martin's nervous illness. 'It was [Papa], wearing over his venerable face, over his white head, the sign of his glorious trial.'[93] Through the humiliation of her father, Thérèse was led to a deeper understanding of the Passion of Christ.

> Like the Adorable Face of Jesus, which was veiled during His Passion, so the face of His faithful servant was to be veiled in the days of his suffering so that it might shine in the Fatherland of Heaven in the presence of his Master, the Eternal Word.[94]

After her father's admission to an asylum in February 1889, Thérèse added the title 'of the Holy Face' to her religious name and turned with new fervour to the devotion to the Holy Face promoted by the Oratory of Tours.[95]

Chesterton, too, was blessed with a remarkable father. E. C. Bentley said that 'family affection', the devotion of his mother and the kindliness of his father, was 'the cradle of that immense benevolence that lived in him'.[96] The father *played* with the son. He was a quietly successful businessman, but the business was not his final goal: his work was a tiresomely necessary interruption of the real business, playing toy theatres with his boys. A man of abundant artistic talents, he never dreamed of 'using them for anything but his own private pleasure and ours ... The old-fashioned Englishman, like my father, sold houses for his living but filled his own house with his life.'[97]

---

[91] See Balthasar, *Schwestern*, p. 114.

[92] MS A, 20rf, OC 100f.

[93] Ibid., 20v, OC 101.

[94] MS A, 20v, OC 101.

[95] 'Jesus burns with love for us ... Look at His lovely Face! ... Look at Jesus in the Face ... There you will see how He loves us. [Signed] Sister Thérèse of the Child Jesus of the Holy Face' (LT 87, to Céline, 4 April 1889, OC 387). See the prayer of 'Consecration à la Sainte Face' (Pri 12, OC 969).

[96] Quoted by Ward, *Return*, p. 17.

[97] *Autobiography*, pp. 35f.

Edward Chesterton was not a Catholic, nor even a properly orthodox Christian, but he did share with Louis Martin this noble accomplishment: he loved his children and protected their innocence. He was what the feminists would have us believe is the rarest of things, a good father. The modern western world seems to have declared war on the family in all its members. It is destructive of the child, disparaging of the mother, and derisive of the father. Feminism, now complacently installed as the worldly wisdom of the West, tends to regard fathers as oppressive monsters in the image of William Blake's Nobodaddy. All that is male, even the masculine pronoun, offends the feminist rulers of this age. Sometimes it seems as if the head of every father is veiled in shame, *un père humiliè*.

The Little Way of St Thérèse and Chesterton, the example of their own actual childhood and their teaching on the spirit of the child, is a divine gift of healing for this culture of parricide. They show the face of a fatherhood which is utterly pure because it is infinitely perfect: the Fatherhood of God the Father revealed by God the Son. The lives and writings of these two prophets inspire 'Confidence in the Father' in a twofold sense. They urge upon us an exercise of the virtue of hope in God the Father, but they also renew our trust in earthly fatherhood, which is a poor but real image of the heavenly (cf. Eph. 3:15). God the Father, through the blood of the Son and the fire of the Spirit, can transform weak men, if they co-operate with His grace, into worthy images of His strong and incandescent paternity.[98]

The Little Way – Exercising the Virtue of Hope

What, then, is the Little Way? First, let us make clear what it is *not*. It is not childishness, the refusal to grow up, that psychological heresy which Chesterton dubbed 'Peter Pantheism'.[99] In the early hours of Christmas Day 1886 Thérèse was given what she called 'the grace of my complete conversion', which was at the same time 'the grace of leaving my

---

[98] Charles Péguy also does much to rekindle confidence in fatherhood, both God's and man's. See ch. 2, passim.
[99] 'Thoughts on Christmas', *The Uses of Diversity* (New York, 1921), p. 222.

childhood'.[100] One might say that she gave up one childhood for another: she left behind natural childhood, which is but a passing state, in order to make more intensely her own the supernatural childhood of her Baptism, the childhood of divine adoption which abides for ever. Here is the paradox of the Gospel. It is only when we convert and become like little children (cf. Matt. 18:3) that we reach our Christian maturity, 'the measure of the age of the fulness of Christ' (cf. Eph. 4:13).

The Little Way is not anti-intellectualism. St Thérèse was a very intelligent young woman. She would not be fobbed off with silly sentiment as a substitute for sound dogma.[101] On the last day of her earthly life, she said, *Oui, il me semble que je n'ai jamais cherché que la vérité*, '… all I have ever sought is the truth'.[102] The Little Way was for her a sure path to the truth.

To be like a child is to have a mind and heart in touch with reality, unobstructed by the fantasies of worldly wisdom. The mysteries of the Kingdom are fittingly revealed to mere babes (cf. Matt. 11:25ff.), because babes, unlike grown-ups who think they know everything, are ready to receive the truth. This is the lesson of Chesterton's early life. It was the memory, or more exactly the maintenance, of his childhood's wonder at existence, his instinctive inclination to be grateful for reality, which woke him up from the nightmare of the Nineties.[103] The child is a realist in the strict metaphysical sense. His wonder is an amazement at what is there.

[100] MS A 45r, OC 141.

[101] See below (pp. 50f.) on the saint's intolerance of foolishly sentimental preaching on Our Lady.

[102] CJ, OC 1144. Reading the conferences of the Abbé Arminjon was, says Thérèse, 'one of the greatest graces of my life': 'All the great truths of religion, the mysteries of eternity, plunged my soul into a happiness that was not that of earth …' (MS A 47v, OC 146).

[103] 'When I had been for some time in these, the darkest depths of the contemporary pessimism, I had a strong inward impulse to revolt; to dislodge this incubus or throw off this nightmare. But as I was still thinking the thing out by myself, with little help from philosophy and no real help from religion, I invented a rudimentary and makeshift mystical theory of my own. It was substantially this: that even mere existence, reduced to its most primary limits, was extraordinary enough to be exciting. Anything was magnificent as compared with nothing. Even if the very daylight were a dream, it was a daydream; it was not a nightmare' (*Autobiography*, pp. 89f.).

Mine is a memory [says Chesterton] of a sort of white light on everything, cutting things out very clearly, and rather emphasizing the solidity. The point is that the white light had a sort of wonder in it, as if the world were as new as myself; but not that the world was anything but a real world.[104]

Till adulthood deceives them, all Toms and Thomasinas are Thomists, philosophers of *esse*, celebrants of the beauty of being. That is why, as Chesterton reminds us, the small child cannot be a pessimist: he 'does not fall into pessimism; he falls into the pond'.[105]

I have defined the Little Way according to the *via negativa*, by saying what it is not. What, in a suitably small nutshell, is its *positive* meaning? Through Mother Agnès, St Thérèse gives us this answer: it is 'the way of spiritual childhood, the path of confidence and total abandonment'.[106] It is an exercise of the Theological Virtue of Hope: trusting and abandoning ourselves, in the manner of a small child, to our heavenly Father. To be little means to resist all temptations to the Nietzschean Will to Power. To have a childlike soul is to remember one's poverty and utter dependence, in all things of nature and grace, upon the heavenly Father. As the saint said to Mother Agnès on the Feast of the Transfiguration 1897:

It means recognizing your nothingness, expecting everything of the good God, just as a little child expects everything of his father.[107]

---

[104] Ibid., pp. 42f.

[105] *The Illustrated London News* (30 May 1908). Chesterton gives a more detailed exposition of the metaphysics of childhood when he is trying to sum up the greatness of the child that was Chaucer: 'There is at the back of all of our lives an abyss of light, more blinding and unfathomable than any abyss of darkness; and it is the abyss of actuality, of existence, of the fact that things truly are, and that we ourselves are incredibly, and sometimes almost incredulously real. It is the fundamental fact of being, as against not being; it is the unthinkable, yet we cannot think it, though we may sometimes be unthinking about it; unthinking and especially unthanking. For he who has realized this reality knows that it does outweigh, literally to infinity, all lesser regrets or arguments for negation, and that under all our grumblings there is a subconscious substance of gratitude' (*Chaucer* [New York, 1932], p. 28).

[106] DE, Other Words to Mother Agnes, OC 1177.

[107] CJ, 6 August 1897, OC 1082.

Here is the first rung on the ladder of humility and therefore the first step towards sanctity, not to mention sanity: the recognition that God is He Who Is, whose very essence is His existence, while we are created out of nothing, receiving our existence from God as a gift.

The Little Way is a practical expression of the dogma of creation, of our dependence upon God for our natural being and activity. But that is not all. It is also the practical expression of the dogma of our *re*-creation, our dependence upon God for our supernatural being and activity. The child of God recognizes that, without God's prevenient grace, merited by the incarnate Son and communicated in the Holy Spirit, he cannot make a single move towards the Father's house in Heaven. Thérèse keeps herself small in order to remember her radical need of God's internal supernatural help, in order to open herself more and more to the movement of the Holy Spirit. Using a metaphor from the 'century of inventions', she says that the Little Way is a 'lift' (*ascenseur*), by which the Holy Spirit can raise Thérèse to Jesus and the Father.

> I am too small to climb the rough stairway of perfection. I searched, then, in the Scriptures for some sign of this elevator, the object of my desires, and I read these words coming from the mouth of Eternal Wisdom: 'Whoever is a little one, let him come to me' (Prov. 9:4) ... [T]he lift to raise me to Heaven is your arms, O Jesus, and for that I have no need to grow up, but rather to stay small, to become smaller and smaller.[108]

The Little Way enables Thérèse to reach the heart of the Church's doctrine of merit. A meritorious act is a grace-filled act and therefore the work of one who, in a childlike way, has opened his heart to the transfiguring action of the Holy Spirit. 'Merit does not consist in doing or giving much, but rather in receiving, in loving much.'[109] There is no need to despair about reaching 'the summit of the mountain of love, because Jesus does not ask for great actions, but only for abandonment and

---

[108] MS C, 3r, OC 237f. Cf. the letter to Seminarian Bellière, where Thérèse says that his soul, like hers, is 'called to rise up to God by the lift of love and not to climb the hard staircase of fear' (LT 258, 18 July 1897, OC 615).

[109] LT 142, to Céline, 6 July 1893, OC 463.

gratitude'.[110] From the summer of 1896, Thérèse's mind turns more and more to the Holy Innocents of Bethlehem and to her own dead little brothers and sisters, who reached Heaven entirely by the grace of Baptism (of Blood in the first case and of Water in the second) without performing any meritorious acts of their own.[111] Thérèse compares herself to them. What has she 'done' in her 'short life'?[112] She *wants* to do great works of charity for Jesus: 'I feel the need, the desire, to accomplish all the most heroic works for you, Jesus.'[113] The trouble is that, when she looks at herself, the thought dawns: 'I have no works!'[114] This does not lead to bitterness or self-pity. Ten years before, her 'little brothers and sisters in Heaven' had set her free from the torment of scruples.[115] Now, in 1896, their example spares her from the fear of approaching Heaven with 'empty hands'. She can even rejoice in her spiritual poverty because 'having nothing, I shall receive everything from the good God'.[116] She, therefore, prays: 'O Holy Innocents, may my palm and my crown be like yours!'[117]

---

[110] LT 196, to Sister Marie of the Sacred Heart, 13 September 1896, OC 550.

[111] As Thérèse makes Our Lady say in the play 'The Flight into Egypt', these little ones are Our Lord's chosen friends and brothers, who have been 'harvested in their innocence' because 'He wants to place them in security and to make them His court of honour' (cf. RP 6, OC 907).

[112] Cf. PN 46, 4.

[113] MS B, 2v, OC 224.

[114] CJ, OC 997.

[115] 'I spoke to them with the simplicity of a child, telling them that, as I was the last in the family, I had always been the most loved, overwhelmed by the affection of my sisters, and that, if they had remained on earth, they would also have given me proofs of affection ... The response was not long in coming. Soon peace began to flood my soul with its delightful waves, and I understood that if I was loved on earth, I was also loved in Heaven ... From that moment my devotion grew for my little brothers and sisters, and I love often to talk with them, to tell them about the sorrows of exile ... and of my desire to go off and join them soon in the heavenly Fatherland' (MS A, 44r, OC 140).

[116] CJ, 23 June 1897, OC 1018.

[117] Pri 18, OC 973. When explaining her Little Way to Mother Agnès, she said: 'I felt I was incapable of earning my living, the eternal life of Heaven. So I have always stayed small. My only occupation is picking flowers, the flowers of love and sacrifice, and offering them to the good God for His pleasure. Being small also means not attributing the virtues you practise to yourself, because you believe you're capable of something, but rather recognizing that the good God places this treasure in the hand of His little child for him to use when he needs to; but it is still the treasure of the good God' (CJ, 6 August 1897, OC 1082).

If the grace of Christ is to bear fruit in holiness, it must trans-figure, through our co-operation, our whole life, our every thought and word and deed. St Thérèse insists that holiness does not consist in extraordinary or extravagant deeds, but in childlike faith, hope, and charity, in glorifying the Trinity and serving our neighbour in the humble circumstances of daily life. It is through 'small sacrifices', she says, that we can help Jesus 'save the souls He has redeemed at the price of His Blood, and which wait for our help not to fall into the abyss'.[118]

The means adopted in the Little Way are modest, but its goal is bold, nothing less than the winning of Heaven. To convert and become like a child is, by small acts, to have a vast and daring hope in the God who is love. This is the heroism of Thérèse: her confidence in the Father's mercy breaks the world's cycle of cynicism and despair. It is seen at its most beautiful in the conversion of Pranzini, her 'first child'. She was convinced that the good God would give *le grand criminel* the grace of repentance if she did but pray, offering up nothing of her own but only 'the infinite merits of Our Lord [and] the treasures of Holy Church'.[119] Likewise, in her play 'The Flight into Egypt', Thérèse has Our Lady say to the mother of the future penitent thief, St Dismas: 'Still have confidence in the infinite mercy of God. It is great enough to efface the greatest crimes when it finds a heart of a mother who places in that mercy all her confidence.'[120] 'What pleases Him', says Thérèse, 'is the blind hope I have in His mercy'.[121]

According to St Thomas Aquinas, in its effect on us, despair, the abandonment of hope, is the gravest of sins.[122] It is the devil's chief weapon of attack. As Chesterton's Father Brown says to Arnold Aylmer when he receives a death-threat: 'These devils always try to make us helpless by making us

---

[118] Letter to Léonie, 12 July 1896, LT 191, OC 543.

[119] MS A, 46r, OC 143.

[120] RP 6, 910.

[121] LT 197, to Sister Marie of the Sacred Heart, OC 552.

[122] 'Through hope', says St Thomas, 'we are called back from evil things and persuaded to pursue good things, and so, once hope is lost, men fall without restraint into vices and are dragged down in their good efforts' (*Summa Theologiae*, 2a2ae 20, 3).

hopeless.'[123] The hope of Thérèse and Chesterton is not a shallow natural buoyancy, but a profound supernatural confidence, the Infused Virtue of Hope, the optimism of the redeemed. For them, as for St Thomas Aquinas, Christian hope is a *Theological* Virtue, Hope in God.[124] It is not for some vaguely defined happiness that they look, but for eternal happiness with Our Lady and the angels and saints in the vision of the Holy Trinity.[125]

False optimism – the optimism, say, of the Victorian worshippers of Progress – tries to prove that man fits into the world: this is the only life he has, and so he had better make the best of it. Christian optimism, by contrast, is based, according to Chesterton, 'on the fact that we do *not* fit into the world'.[126] The hope for a final resting-place in Heaven does not make this world seem monotonous and stale; on the contrary, it makes it all the more marvellous and strange. The supernatural hope perfects the natural hope of the child, as Chesterton goes on to explain:

> The modern philosopher had told me again and again that I was in the right place, and I had still felt depressed even in acquiescence. But I had heard that I was in the *wrong* place, and my soul sang for joy, like a bird in Spring. The knowledge found out and illuminated forgotten chambers in the dark house of infancy. I knew now why grass had always seemed to me as queer as the green beard of a giant, and why I could feel homesick at home.[127]

Chesterton's Distributism is an application of the Little Way to economics and politics. It is the defence of childhood in a twofold sense. First, its goal is the protection of natural childhood, of actual children, the sons and daughters of husbands and wives. The widespread distribution of property is but a means to an end, and that end is the flourishing of the family, of fathers and mothers and their children.[128] Secondly, the spirit

[123] Chesterton, 'The Dagger with Wings' in *The Incredulity of Father Brown* (New York, 1926), p. 184.

[124] Cf. St Thomas Aquinas, *Summa Theologiae*, 2a2ae 17, 5.

[125] Ibid., 17, 2.

[126] Chesterton, *Orthodoxy* (New York and London, 1909), p. 146.

[127] Ibid., pp. 146f.

[128] A just wage, according to Pope Leo XIII, can be defined as a wage sufficient to enable a man comfortably to support his wife, his children, and himself (*Rerum novarum*, n. 46).

of Distributism is a childlike spirit, summed up by a more recent author in the surprising aphorism and successful title *Small is Beautiful*.[129] When more and more men become small owners, then fewer men are likely to be Big Owners. When Solidarity is happily married to Subsidiarity, when society is centred on the humility of the home, men will be somewhat fortified against the temptations of Promethean and Pelagian pride. The colossal combinations of the Capitalist Corporation and the Socialist State are structural occasions of sin, likely to lead the business-man or bureaucrat to rely on his own merely human strengths and achievements, and the ordinary citizen to despair of his powerlessness. Distributism keeps a man faithful to what is smallest and most precious – his family, his wife and children. It helps the sons of Adam resist the Will to Power and the worship of the State. It is an implicit devotion to the Holy Family, presenting the stark choice, as Vincent McNabb put it, between Nazareth and Social Chaos.[130]

Chesterton drew upon the philosophy of Distributism in his passionate defence of human life against that practical hatred of the child which is Birth Control. The contraceptive mentality is a typical product of the Servile Society for whose overthrow the distributist struggles. 'My contempt', said Chesterton, 'boils over into bad behavior when I hear the common suggestion that a birth is avoided because people want to be "free" to go to the cinema or buy a gramophone.'[131] By preferring these material amusements, they chain themselves to Capitalism, 'the most servile and mechanical system yet tolerated by men',[132] and reject that which is 'the very sign and sacrament of personal freedom ... a fresh will added to the wills of the world' – the child.[133] 'They are preferring the last, crooked, indirect, borrowed, repeated, and exhausted things of our dying Capitalist civilization, to the reality which is the only rejuvenation of all

[129] See E. F. Schumacher, *Small is Beautiful. A Study of Economics as if People Mattered* (London, 1973).

[130] Cf. *Nazareth or Social Chaos* (London, 1933).

[131] 'Babies and Distributism', in *The Well and the Shallows* in *The Collected Works of G. K. Chesterton*, vol. 3 (San Francisco, 1990), p. 440.

[132] Ibid.

[133] Ibid., p. 441.

civilization.'[134] Contraceptive Capitalism is a culture of use and therefore of death, a society ordered to lifeless things and their consumption. The civilization of love is a culture of life, a society ordered towards marriage and the family and therefore ever open to the influx of youth.

The Little Way – Living the Grace of Baptism

St Thérèse and Chesterton teach us that we poor tired sons of Adam need to be made young again. We have to turn and become like children if we are to enter the Kingdom. But we cannot do so by the techniques of psychology (by 'getting in touch with the Inner Child' in the manner of the New Agers), nor indeed by any unaided human effort. Men have to be reborn from above, as children *of God*, by water and the Holy Spirit (cf. John 3:3ff.) – as Thérèse was in the baptistery of Notre Dame in Alençon and Chesterton in the font of St George's Campden Hill (not, as he carefully pointed out, in the Waterworks Tower facing the church).

In the Sacrament of Baptism the sons of Adam are given second birth, the grace of sonship-in-the-Son of God. The Little Way is nothing other than the living out of that baptismal grace, its translation into daily existence. While looking after some small children before her entry to Carmel, Thérèse suddenly realized the immensity of the supernatural powers placed in the souls of baptized infants – the powers of Sanctifying Grace, the Infused Virtues, and the Gifts of the Holy Spirit. The simplicity of the children's questions about 'Little Jesus and His beautiful Heaven' was an effect of their Baptism; grace had perfected the natural unaffectedness of their minds. 'Holy Baptism', Thérèse concluded, 'must plant a very deep seed of the Theological Virtues in souls, since from childhood those Virtues are already evident, and the hope of future goods is enough to make [children] accept sacrifices.'[135] In one of her poems, she says, addressing Our Lady of Victories, that the 'holy water of Baptism' makes the

[134] Ibid.
[135] MS A, 52v, OC 156.

baby of one day a temple where God Himself 'deigns to dwell in love'.[136]

But the miracle of spiritual childhood does not end there. When adult sins strip us of the baptismal innocence of our infancy, the risen Jesus, through the Sacrament of Penance, re-clothes and rejuvenates us in the divine life of His grace. In his *Autobiography* Chesterton confesses that he became a Catholic to get rid of his sins, for, as he saw it, no other religious body had, or even claimed, power from the God-Man to remit sins. This astonishing Sacrament, says Chesterton, is a regular return to childhood.

> [The Catholic] believes that in that dim corner, and in that brief ritual, God has really remade him in His own image. He is now a new experiment of the Creator. He is as much a new experiment as he was when he was really only five years old. He stands ... in the white light at the worthy beginning of the life of a man. The accumulations of time can no longer terrify. He may be grey and gouty, but he is only five minutes old.[137]

2. Playing with the Son

The Little Way – Devotion to Christ and Christmas

The Little Way is a devotion to God the Son in all the mysteries of His divinity and humanity, but above all in His human infancy, in the mystery of Christmas. The Son came from the Father by the Little Way, as a child, and by the Little Way, as children, we are led by Him to the Father. This is the

---

[136] PN 35, 'A Notre Dame des Victoires, Reine des Vierges, des Apôtres et des Martyrs', OC 719.

[137] Chesterton, *Autobiography*, p. 341. For Chesterton, converting to the Catholic Church truly meant converting and becoming like a little child. In a letter to Monsignor Ronald Knox, explaining his spiritual struggle, he made this admission: 'I am concerned about what has become of a little boy whose father showed him a toy theatre, and a schoolboy whom nobody ever heard of, with his brooding on doubts and dirt and day-dreams of crude conscientiousness so inconsistent as to [be] near to hypocrisy; and all the morbid life of the lonely mind of a living person with whom I have lived. It is that story, that so often came near to ending badly, that I want to end well' (cited in Joseph Pearce, *Wisdom and Innocence. The Life of G. K. Chesterton* [San Francisco, 1996], p. 264).

direct connection between Lisieux and Beaconsfield: they
are both on the main line to Bethlehem. St Thérèse is Sister
Thérèse of the Child Jesus. Had GKC belonged to the OCD, he,
too, would doubtless have been Brother Gilbert of the Child
Jesus.

If one were to make a collection of Chesterton's Christmas
writings (it has still not been done), it would be a fittingly fat
and jolly volume. It would gather up all the annual Christmas
articles for the newspapers, the eulogies of the great Christmases
of fiction (especially in Dickens),[138] the pages on 'The God in
the Cave' in *The Everlasting Man*, and above all the poems: 'A
Christmas Carol' (two of them), 'A Christmas Rhyme', 'The
House of Christmas', 'Christmas Day', 'Gloria in Profundis'.[139]
A Thérèse Christmas anthology would include, among other
things, the plays written for Christmas recreation: 'The Angels
at the Crib of Jesus', 'The Divine Little Beggar of Christmas',
'The Flight into Egypt'.[140]

Thérèse had happy memories of the Christmases of her
childhood. In a poem dedicated to Céline she says:

> I loved each year to place
> My slipper by the chimney.
> I rushed down as soon as I awoke,
> I sang the feast of Heaven –
> Christmas![141]

The Christmas chimney: it is Catholic Normandy's form of the
English 'flaming hearth' so often praised by Chesterton.[142]

As I mentioned earlier, it was by the beloved Christmas hearth
that Thérèse received the grace of her conversion in 1886. A
'wonderful exchange' took place that night: the eternal Son of
the Father who had become the little child of the Virgin made

---

[138] Of *The Christmas Carol*, Chesterton says: 'The Christmas atmosphere is
more important than Scrooge, or the ghosts either' (*Charles Dickens* [London,
1906], p. 122).
[139] See Mackey, pp. 104, 125, 126, 128, 137, 139.
[140] OC 801ff., 873ff., 887ff.
[141] PN 18, 'The Hymn of Céline', OC 672.
[142] See the essay 'Yule Log and Democrat' in *The Uses of Diversity*, pp.
214ff.

the child of Louis and Zélie Martin grow up into His own fulness of age.[143] Much later she says:

> The night of Christmas 1886 was, it's true, decisive for my vocation, but to name it more exactly I should call it 'the night of my conversion'. On that blessed night, of which it is written that 'it illumines God's delights', Jesus, who became a child for me, deigned to bring me forth from the swaddling clothes and imperfections of childhood. He transformed me so much that I no longer recognized myself.[144]

Like the medieval Doctors before her, St Thérèse held the view that the Son of God first preached the message of His adulthood ('Unless you become like a little child ...') by the fact of His own childhood.[145] By becoming the child of the Virgin, the eternal Son of the Father raises all natural childhood to a new and wonderful dignity and opens up for us the way of spiritual childhood, as adopted children of God.

> Hark! Laughter like a lion wakes
> To roar to the resounding plain,
> And the whole Heaven shouts and shakes,
> For God Himself is born again,
> And we are little children walking
>   Through the snow and rain ...
>
> Have a myriad children been quickened,
> Have a myriad children grown old,
> Grown gross and unloved and embittered,
> Grown cunning and savage and cold?
> God abides in a terrible patience,
> Unangered, unworn,
> And again for the child that was squandered
>   A child is born.[146]

---

[143] 'From this moment she stops crying. Her mind is healed. She regains her self-control' (Father Marie-Eugène OCD, *Ton amour a grandi avec moi*, p. 38).

[144] LT 201, to Father Roulland in China, 1 November 1896, OC 559.

[145] For example, Blessed Guerric of Igny praises the newborn Christ with these words: 'O sweet and holy childhood, who hast restored true innocence to men, through whom every age may return to blessed childhood and be conformed to thee, not in brevity of limbs, but in humility of mind and piety of manners' (*Sermo 1 in nativitate Domini* 2; SC 166. 168).

[146] 'The Wise Men' and 'The Nativity', in Mackey, pp. 129, 139.

The Little Way of confidence and abandonment is a kind of Christmas game, playing with the Child Jesus in the presence of the Father, or rather it is a willingness to let the Infant God play with us. 'I am the little Ball of the Child Jesus; if He wants to break His toy, He is free to do so. I want all He wants.'[147] Suddenly all nights of sense and spirit are protected from Stoic or Jansenistic grimness. There is silence – Jesus is playing hide-and-seek. It is dark – the Child Jesus is asleep.[148]

The imagery of play is most important. According to St Thomas Aquinas, following Aristotle, playfulness is a natural virtue and too little play a vice.[149] Since grace presupposes and perfects nature, it would seem to follow that our divinized life in Christ must include a supernaturalized play. That is certainly Balthasar's view in his study of St Thérèse:

> While the grown-up groans beneath the curse of the toil that comes from Original Sin, the child busies himself with play, which originates in Paradise and is a creaturely reflection of God's creative busy-ness. God is at play with men; that is, He handles them in a divine fashion, according to His own laws – for there are none higher.[150]

Maisie Ward records a beautiful moment in the playing career of Chesterton. He had been invited to make a speech at a children's Nativity Play in Princes' Risborough. During the interval he gently played with a baby sitting on his mother's lap. 'He's waiting for his cue to go on stage', said the mother proudly, 'He is the Child Jesus!' '"Am I really allowed to play

[147] LT 36, 20 November 1887, after her audience with Pope Leo XIII, when she felt so desolate, OC 329. In her autobiography, having described her disappointment following the audience with the Pope, she says: 'For some time I had offered myself to the Child Jesus to be His little toy' (MS A, 64r, OC 177). Again, in her play 'The Divine Little Beggar of Christmas', she says: 'Do you want to be on earth / The toy of the Divine Child? / My sister, do you wish to please Him? / Remain in His small hand' (RP 5, 879).

[148] Meritorious acts are not a solemn, self-conscious heroism: she acts, she says, 'not to gain merits, but to give pleasure to Jesus' (cf. LT 143, to Céline, 18 July 1893, OC 467).

[149] Cf. *Summa theologiae*, 2a2ae 168, 2 & 4.

[150] Balthasar, *Schwestern*, p. 281.

with the Child Jesus?" asked G.K. simply, and was instantly and completely absorbed.'[151]

The Little Way – The Way of Orthodox Faith in Christ

The Little Way is the way of orthodox faith in Christ, the faith defended and expounded by the great Ecumenical Councils from Nicaea I to Nicaea II. Neither St Thérèse nor Chesterton forget that what raises human childhood up to a new dignity is its assumption by a Divine Person, One of the Trinity, true God from true God.[152] He who was born in time in His humanity of the Virgin Mother is the Son begotten eternally in His divinity of the heavenly Father. The baby in the cave is God. Thérèse sings of the 'Word made child' (*Verbe fait enfant*).[153] In one of her Christmas plays, she muses: 'Who, then, can understand this mystery, / A God makes Himself a little child?'[154]

In the chorus from an unfinished play, 'Gloria in Profundis' (superbly illustrated by Eric Gill), Chesterton likewise speaks of 'a God too great for the sky' falling to earth:[155] 'a thing unending / Has slipped into space and is small'.[156] It was for these dogmatic reasons that he was intolerant of any puritanical diminishing of the Christmastide festivities. In *The Everlasting Man*, he points out that the very merriment of the feast can be an apologetic for orthodoxy:

> Any agnostic or atheist whose childhood has known a real Christmas has ever afterwards, whether he likes it or not, an association in his mind between two ideas that most of mankind must regard as remote from each other; the idea of a baby and the idea of the unknown strength that sustains the stars.[157]

[151] Ward, *Return*, pp. 241f.
[152] See Father Léthel's remarks about Thérèse's presentation of Jesus as One of the Trinity in her 'Act of Oblation' (op. cit., pp. 510f.).
[153] Cf. 'Les Anges à la Crèche de Jésus', RP 2, OC 801.
[154] RP 2, 'Les Anges à la Crèche de Jésus', Christmas Day 1894, OC 802. In the play 'The Mission of Joan of Arc' (January 1894), Thérèse makes St Margaret say: 'Jesus, the Son of the living God, / Has veiled His ineffable glory / Beneath the traits of a little child' (RP 1, 790).
[155] Mackey, p. 137.
[156] Typescript earlier version of last stanza of 'Gloria in profundis', Mackey, p. 138n.
[157] *The Everlasting Man*, in *The Collected Works of G. K. Chesterton*, vol. 2, p. 302.

Both St Thérèse and Chesterton remember that human childhood, human life, begins for the Son of God, as it does for us, in the *womb*. This is expressed beautifully in one of Thérèse's most important poems, 'Jésus, mon Bien-Aimé, rappelle-toi!', 'Jesus, my beloved, remember!'

> Remember the glory of the Father
> Remember the divine splendours
> That you left when you went into exile on earth
> To redeem all poor sinners
> O Jesus, in self-abasement towards the Virgin Mary
> You veiled your grandeur and infinite glory
>   Ah, remember your Mother's womb,
>   Which was your second heaven.[158]

Chesterton often lingered over the beauty and vulnerability of unborn human life. In one mysterious poem, dating from the year of Thérèse's death, he speaks in the person of a 'Babe Unborn'. It is as if the child, through Chesterton, were pleading with our century:

> I think that if they gave me leave
>   Within the world to stand,
> I would be good through all the day
>   I spent in fairyland.
>
> They should not hear a word from me
>   Of selfishness or scorn,
> If only I could find the door,
>   If only I were born.[159]

In speaking of the Crib, Thérèse never forgets the Cross. After her father's admission to the asylum, she becomes 'Sister Thérèse of the Child Jesus of the Holy Face'. The very name articulates one of her insights: the inseparability of Christmas and Easter. She sees the Crib in the Cross and the Cross in the Crib, as Charles Péguy did: 'Life inscribed between Bethlehem and Jerusalem.'[160]

---

[158] PN 241, OC 692.
[159] 'By the Babe Unborn', Mackey, p. 198.
[160] Cf. *Mystère*, OPC 75.

In the play 'The Angels at the Crib of Jesus', the Angel of the Holy Face brings the Angel of the Child Jesus the instruments of the Passion and Veronica's veil with the Holy Face,[161] while another unfurls the flag of the Resurrection:

> This helpless child
> One day will be mighty
> He will rise again
> For ever He will reign.[162]

The Little Flower recognizes that, from the Virgin Mary's undefiled womb to Joseph of Arimathea's unused tomb, the Son followed one consistent line of love for the Father and for us.

Thérèse took as her motto the two extreme moments of Jesus' life. In the light of these two extremes, the mystery of the God-Man unfolds before her eyes. Together they manifest the same fundamental attitude of the Son with regard to the Father and with regard to mankind: nakedness, abandonment, vulnerability.[163]

The Little Way – Living the Grace of the Eucharist

In the womb of the Virgin, without ceasing to be infinitely great in His divinity, the eternal Son became a tiny unborn child in our humanity. In the mystery of the Holy Eucharist, without local movement, the same Son – Body, Blood, Soul, and Divinity – becomes substantially present under the tiny form of a wafer. On the altar, says Thérèse, the Author of Life becomes 'even smaller than a child'.[164] Like St Francis of Assisi, Thérèse sees the Real Presence as a continuation of the 'Little Way' that the Son of God took on His journey to us in the Incarnation. Thérèse wants to respond to the loving foolishness of Incarnation and Eucharist by making herself an 'atom' before the tabernacle.

> I am only a speck of dust,
> But I want to settle down
> In the shadows of the sanctuary
> With the Prisoner of Love

[161] RP 2, OC 804ff.
[162] Ibid., 808.
[163] Hans Urs von Balthasar, 'The Timeliness of Lisieux', *Carmelite Studies* (1980), 113.
[164] RP 2, 'Les Anges à la Crèche de Jésus', OC 809.

Ah, to the Host my soul aspires
I love Him and want nothing more
It is the hidden God who draws me,
I am the atom of Jesus.[165]

Father François-Marie Léthel OCD has described this as
Thérèse's entry 'into the most complete and intimate communion with the extreme smallness of Jesus in the mysteries of
His humanity'.[166] The *res sacramenti* of the Eucharist, the fruit of
a worthy Communion, is the completion of our incorporation
into Christ, a perfected union with the God-Man and the other
members of His Mystical Body. Thérèse's mysticism is built
upon this solid dogmatic foundation: she wants to be little in
humility, through her union with Jesus humbly present in the
littleness of the Host, so that she can be great in charity at the
heart of the Church.[167]

In his poem 'Lepanto', Chesterton suggests another effect of
the Little Way of the Eucharist: those who worship the great
God in the Host are likely to see the world He created in its
proper proportions. The Pope's chapel of the Blessed Sacrament
is not only the 'hidden room in a man's house where God sits
all the year' but also 'the secret window whence the world looks
small and very dear'.[168] The Little Way provides the long view.[169]

3. Soldiering in the Spirit

The Little Way – Living the Grace of Confirmation

St Thérèse received the Sacrament of Confirmation on Saturday
14 June 1884 at the hands of Bishop Flavien Hugonin of Bayeux.
She prepared herself with great care: 'I couldn't understand',
she says, 'why people didn't give much attention to the reception

---

[165] PN 19, 'L'atome de Jésus-Hostie', OC 682.
[166] Léthel, p. 495.
[167] See pp. 48f. below.
[168] Mackey, p. 551.
[169] Thirteen years after the death of St Thérèse, through the decree *Quam
singulari* of the Sacred Congregation of the Sacraments, Pope St Pius X restored
Holy Communion to the young children of the Latin Church, so that 'children,
even from their tender years, may be united to Jesus Christ, may live His life,
and obtain protection from all dangers of corruption' (AAS 2 [1910], 582ff.).

of this Sacrament of Love.'[170] The Little Flower took two days to prepare herself for Confirmation:

> Oh, how joyful was my soul, as I waited happily, like the Apostles, for the visit of the Holy Spirit ... I rejoiced at the thought that soon I would be a complete Christian, and above all that I would bear eternally on my forehead the mysterious cross that the Bishop imprints as he confers the Sacrament ... At last the happy moment arrived. When the Holy Spirit came down, I didn't feel a rushing wind but rather the light breeze that the prophet Elias heard on Mount Horeb ... On that day I received the strength to *suffer*, for soon afterwards the martyrdom of my soul was about to begin.[171]

With her customary dogmatic accuracy, St Thérèse presents Confirmation as a Sacrament of Martyrdom. She learnt from her catechism that, through the Sacrament of Chrism, the baptized are strengthened by the Holy Spirit 'to resist all the assaults of the world, the flesh, and the Devil, while their minds are fully confirmed in faith to confess and glorify the name of Our Lord Jesus Christ',[172] a strengthening by the Holy Spirit for Christian witness in a hostile world. The bishop gently slapped her on the cheek, making her recall that 'as a valiant combatant, [she] should be prepared to endure with unconquered spirit all adversities for the name of Christ'.[173] When the bishop traced the 'mysterious cross' on her forehead, an indelible character was impressed upon her soul.[174] The adopted daughter of the Father was now marked out as a conscript of Christ, a soldier in the Holy Spirit.

The Little Way is a devotion to God the Holy Spirit, the living out of the grace He gives in Confirmation. It is the way the soldiers of Christ march to war. Those who are most childlike towards Jesus and the Father are the most militant towards the world and the Devil. Lambs-in-the-Lamb will be

---

[170] MS A, 36v, OC 127.
[171] Ibid., OC 128.
[172] *Catechism of the Council of Trent for Parish Priests*. Issued by Order of Pope Pius V (ET New York and London, 1934), p. 209.
[173] Ibid., pp. 211f.
[174] Ibid., p. 210.

lions-in-the-Lion towards the Serpent.[175] They will follow the Lamb wherever He goes and co-operate in all His works, even unto the Harrowing of Hell. Their 'wrestling is not against flesh and blood, but against principalities and powers ... against the spirits of wickedness in the high places' (Eph. 6:12). They overcome the Accuser of the Brethren 'by the blood of the Lamb and by the word of the testimony, and they loved not their lives unto death' (Apoc. 12:10f.).

Thérèse's warrior soul flashes forth on every page of her writings. In a poem addressed to the martyr of Tonkin, Théophane Vénard, she asks for help in her spiritual battle:

> Soldier of Christ, lend me your weapons
> On behalf of sinners, here below I want
> To struggle, to suffer in the shadow of your palms
> Protect me, come to support my arm.
> For them, by unceasing warfare,
> I want to take by violence the Kingdom of God
> For the Lord brought on earth
> Not peace, but the Sword and Fire![176]

The entry into Carmel was not a fearful retreat from the battles of the Church but a bold advance to the front. 'Sanctity! It has to be won at the point of the sword.'[177] Balthasar's words may shock us, but they paint a faithful portrait of Thérèse: 'She loves *war*. She is by nature a fighter.'[178] 'God has granted me', she says, 'the grace not to fear the battle; I must do my duty at all costs.'[179] During her postulancy, she discovered Our Lord's

---

[175] '[Christ] is great Lion through His divinity, little Lamb through His humanity, Lion through the power of His majesty, Lamb through His meekness, Lion in punishing the wicked, Lamb in redeeming the good, Lion in fortitude, Lamb in devotion' (Richard of St Victor, *In Apocalypsim Ioannis*, lib. 2; PL 196. 756D).

[176] PN 47, 'À Théophane Vénard', OC 738.

[177] LT 89, to Céline, 26 April 1889, OC 390. Towards the end of her life, in a letter to Father Roulland, she said: 'God wanted to make me conquer the fortress of Carmel at the sword's point' (LT 201, 1 November 1896, OC 560).

[178] Balthasar, *Schwestern*, pp. 227f.

[179] MS C, 23v, OC 266. In her final illness, she told Mother Agnès how she had dreamt that soldiers were needed for a war. 'You said: We must send Sister Thérèse of the Child Jesus. I replied that I should have preferred it to be

words in St Matthew's Gospel: 'I came not to bring peace but a sword' (Matt. 10:34). In a letter to Céline she commented: 'There remains nothing else for us to do but to fight, and when we don't have the strength, it is then that Jesus fights for us.'[180] At the end, in August 1897, she said with the defiance of a battle-scarred warrior: 'I shall die with weapons in hand.'[181]

As a child, like St Teresa, Thérèse loved to read stories of chivalry and throughout her life had an enthusiastic devotion to the soldier-saint of France, Joan of Arc.[182] She composed two poems and two plays in Joan's honour; indeed, she took the part of Joan when the plays were performed in Carmel as *récréations pieuses*.[183] In her autobiography she tells Our Lord: 'Like Joan of Arc, my dearest sister, I should like at the stake to murmur your name, O Jesus.'[184] In a prayer inspired by a picture of Joan she says:

Lord God of armies, you said in your Gospel, 'I came to bring not peace but a sword'. Arm me for the struggle. I yearn to fight for your glory, but I beg you, strengthen my courage ...[185]

In an exhilarating passage in *Orthodoxy*, Chesterton exercises his own chivalry in defence of the chivalry of Joan. With one sweep of his sword, he cuts to shreds Anatole France's sceptical tract, *Jeanne d'Arc*: 'It discredits supernatural stories that have some foundation, simply by telling natural stories that have no foundation. Because we cannot believe in what a saint did, we are to pretend that we know exactly what he felt.'[186] Chesterton

for a holy war. In the end, I went anyway. Oh no, I would not have been afraid to go to war. How happy I'd have been, say at the time of the Crusades, to have gone off to fight the heretics. I wouldn't have been afraid to get a bullet!' (CJ, 4 August 1897, OC 1076f.).

[180] LT 57, 23 July 1888, OC 350f.
[181] CJ, 9 August 1997, OC 1086.
[182] See MS A, 32r, OC 119.
[183] PN 4, 'Cantique pour obtenir la canonisation de la Vénérable Jeanne d'Arc', OC 642ff.; PN 50, 'À Jeanne d'Arc', OC 743ff.; RP 1, 'La Mission de Jeanne d'Arc', OC 775ff.; RP 3, 'Jeanne d'Arc accomplissant sa Mission', OC 819ff.
[184] MS B, 3r, OC 225.
[185] Pri 17, 'Prière inspirée par une image représentant la Vénérable Jeanne d'Arc', OC 972.
[186] *Orthodoxy*, p. 77.

goes on to show how serenely the Maid of Orleans surpasses the sages and supermen of the Nineties:

> Joan of Arc was not stuck at the cross-roads, either by rejecting all the paths like Tolstoy, or by accepting them all like Nietzsche. *She chose a path, and went down it like a thunderbolt* ... She beat them both at their antagonistic ideals; she was more gentle than the one, more violent than the other. Yet she was a perfectly practical person who did something, while they are wild speculators who do nothing.[187]

Joan is a little maiden, *la Pucelle*, and yet she is a soldier, the marshal of the hosts of France. There is no contradiction. The smallest and frailest of all has opened herself, without reserve, to the strengthening grace of the Holy Spirit, and so she can be the sturdiest and bravest of all. For Joan and for Thérèse, the 'Little Way' is a sword of the Spirit for their spiritual war against Satan and the world. In one of the plays on St Joan, Thérèse makes St Michael say:

> The day of victory is coming,
> The day that will save the kingdom of the Franks.
> But to God alone belongs all the glory.
> To prove it, He arms the arm of a child ...[188]

He arms the arm of a child ... This was Our Lord's message to St Paul in his weakness: 'My grace is sufficient for thee; for power is made perfect in infirmity' (2 Cor. 12:9). To convert and become like a little child is to drop the barriers of pride that block the empowering mission of the Holy Spirit. Confirmed by the Spirit, the little child of the Father becomes the fiercest soldier of Christ. In the mid-Nineties Chesterton summarized this argument in a poem:

> When earth and all her seers were sad
> The child rose from the floor
> He tossed his newspaper cocked hat
> And drumming, passed the door.

---

[187] Ibid., pp. 78f. Monsignor Ronald Knox once said of St Thérèse in a sermon: 'Her life, so short, was so businesslike; she cut out all the frills' (*Occasional Sermons* [London, 1960], p. 92).

[188] RP 1, 'La Mission de Jeanne d'Arc', OC 780f.

> His crest was but a feather, such
>   For seraph' wing sufficed:
> His sword was but a cross of wood:
>   So was the cross of Christ ...
>
> Not for years was the idle child
>   Seen by his peoples' eyes,
> But strange things done in a distant sea
>   Came to the ears of the wise.
>
> And the sages stared and ceased to weep –
>   In the dawn of an ancient light
> For the dragon that ate the sun and moon
>   Lay dead by the seas of night.[189]

The Little Way – Love in the Heart of the Church

Thérèse's Little Way is a way of spiritual warfare, but first of all it is the way of love of God and neighbour. The Spirit who strengthens her to be a soldier for Christ is the Spirit who pours the Theological Virtue of Charity into her heart (cf. Rom. 5:5). The Holy Spirit is the Love of the Father and the Son: in Him They love each other and us, and in Him we love Them and one another.[190] Thus Thérèse prays:

> Ah, Divine Jesus, you know I love you.
> The Spirit of Love sets me ablaze with His fire.[191]

Charity, love – this is the Little Flower's vocation:

> I realized that *Love* contained all Vocations ... So, overflowing with delirious joy, I cried out, 'O Jesus, my Love ... at last I have found my vocation. My vocation is Love! ... Yes, I have found my place in the Church, and that place, O my God, is the one you gave me ... *In the heart of the Church, my Mother, I will be Love* ... That way I shall be everything ... So my dream will come true!'[192]

---

[189] 'The Child', in Mackey, pp. 198f.

[190] Cf. St Thomas Aquinas, *Summa theologiae*, 1a 37, 2.

[191] Cf. PN 17, 'Vivre d'Amour', OC 667.

[192] MS B, 3v, OC 226. Father François-Marie Léthel OCD offers this commentary on the same passage: 'Thérèse discovers that the Heart of the Church is the place *par excellence* of the Holy Spirit in the Church. This Heart is burning with love because it always contains all the fire of Pentecost ... The Heart that

For the love of Christ, the saints fight for Christ. As St Joan says in one of Thérèse's plays, 'I want to fight for Jesus ... / To win for Him souls without number / I want to love Him more and more!'[193] The acts of charity of the saints coincide with their acts of spiritual combat. This is the lofty doctrine of the *De Civitate Dei* of St Augustine, who argues that human history is an epic struggle between two cities and their respective loves: love of self (in the earthly city) leading to disregard of God and love of God (in the heavenly city) leading to disregard of self.[194] Through her co-redemptive love in the heart of the Church, by reaching out to the Scepticism, Pessimism, and Egoism of the Nineties with her heroic Faith, Hope, and Charity, Thérèse defeats the alliance of unlove – the world, the flesh, and the Devil.

We can now see what Balthasar means when he describes St Thérèse's Little Way as 'the demolition of bogus religion'.

The Baptist, by the Jordan, in the spirit of Elias, clears the ground to give the approaching Messiah room and air. This blazing passion is itself only a preparation for the absolute passion with which the Son flattens every obstacle to the Father's glory. 'Whoever draws near me draws near fire', so runs one of Our Lord's apocryphal sayings, and indeed each of His words and works and wonders is fire, a fire all the more consuming because it is not the fire of justice but of love. And once Christ has cast this fire on earth, He sends His saints to fan it into flame so that it cannot be damped down in the hearths of a 'bourgeois' Christianity.[195]

Balthasar then points us to the target of Thérèse's swords-manship:

---

burns with Love is first of all the Heart of Jesus, but it is also the Heart of the Church, the Bride of Jesus, in her most intimate union with Him, because Jesus, at Pentecost, gave the Church all the fire of the Holy Spirit who burned within His Heart. This fire, having burned away all the sin of the world in the darkness of Calvary, makes His body for ever resplendent in the Resurrection' (Léthel, *Connaître*, p. 553).

[193] RP 3, 'Jeanne d'Arc accomplissant sa Mission', OC 835.

[194] *De Civitate Dei*, 14, 28; CCSL 48. 451.

[195] Balthasar, *Schwestern*, p. 227.

Her battle is to wipe out the hard core of Pharisaism that stubbornly persists in the midst of the New Covenant: man's Will-to-Power using religion as a means to an end, the will for one's own greatness in place of the greatness of God, who alone is great.[196]

The Little Way is one long war against Antichrist, the definitive answer to Zarathustra and sanity for the soul of Nietzsche. Spiritual childhood is a wild knighthood.

> So, with the wan waste grasses on my spear,
> I ride for ever, seeking after God.
> My hair grows whiter than my thistle plume,
> And all my limbs are loose; but in my eyes
> The star of an unconquerable praise:
> For in my soul one hope for ever sings,
> That at the next white corner of a road
> My eyes may look on Him ...[197]

4. More Mother than Queen

The Little Way is Our Lady's way. It is the way she follows, the way she *is*. By the working of the Spirit, the Son came to us from the Father along the Little Way, as a child of Mary, and as children of Mary, along the Little Way, by the working of the Spirit, the Son now leads us to the Father.

The Little Way – Our Lady as Motherly Model

The Blessed Virgin followed her Son to the Father by the Little Way of Spiritual Childhood. St Thérèse once confessed to Mother Agnès that none of the sermons she had heard about Our Lady had ever touched her. The *fervorini* made the Virgin grandiose rather than truly great, ascribing to her extravagant privileges beyond those determined by the Church's dogmas.[198]

---

[196] Ibid., p. 231.

[197] 'The Wild Knight', G. K. Chesterton, *The Collected Poems*, new edition (New York, 1932), p. 350.

[198] For example, the idea that Our Lady did not experience any physical sufferings, or that when she was presented in the Temple at the age of three, she offered herself to God with 'ardent and quite extraordinary sentiments of love, whereas she probably went quite simply to obey her parents' (CJ, 21 August 1897, OC 1103).

Thérèse had a very clear idea of what was needed: 'For a sermon to please me and do me some good, I need to see [Our Lady's] real life, not her supposed life; and I am sure that her real life must have been very simple.'[199] She wanted priests to present her 'practicable virtues'. 'It is good to speak of her prerogatives, but above all we need to be able to imitate her. She prefers imitation to admiration, and her life was so simple.'[200]

> Of course, the Blessed Virgin is Queen of Heaven and Earth, but she is more Mother than Queen, and we must not say that because of her privileges she eclipses the glory of all the saints, as the sun on its rising makes the stars disappear. *Mon Dieu!* How strange that would be! A Mother who made the glory of her children disappear![201]

The Mother of God shares her all with us. She is immaculately generous with the graces of her heart. In Thérèse's last and greatest poem, *Pourquoi je t'aime, ô Marie*, she shows her familiarity with the doctrine of St Louis de Montfort, who said that, when we receive Jesus in Holy Communion, the Blessed Virgin is ready to lend us her heart to welcome Him:

> The mother's treasure belongs to the child,
> And I am your child, Mother dear,
> Your virtues, your love, are they not mine?
> So when the white Host descends into my heart
> Jesus, your sweet Lamb, thinks He's resting in you![202]

For St Thérèse, again as for St Louis de Montfort, Our Lady is *la petite Marie*,[203] the purest embodiment of the little way of union with Christ by faith, hope, and charity.[204] Our Lord's Handmaid

---

[199] Ibid.
[200] CJ, 23 August 1897, OC 1107.
[201] CJ, 21 August 1897, OC 1103.
[202] PN 54, OC 751.
[203] 'The Incomprehensible let Himself be comprehended and completely contained by little Mary, without losing any of His immensity; and it is also by little Mary that we must let ourselves be contained and perfectly guided without any reserve' (St Louis-Marie Grignion de Montfort, *Traité de la vraie dévotion à la Sainte Vierge*, n. 157, *Oeuvres complètes* [Paris, 1966], p. 586).
[204] See de Meester, *Dynamique de la confiance*, pp. 382ff.

follows Him along the ordinary path, in her humble daily life. The grandeur of the Mother of God is her littleness.[205] The great Queen of Heaven is the lowly Handmaid of the Lord.

> You make me feel it's not impossible
> To follow in your footsteps, O Queen of the Elect,
> The narrow way to Heaven you have made visible
> By always practising the humblest virtues,
> Close to you, Mary, I like to stay small,
> I see the vanity of worldly grandeur ...[206]

> In Nazareth, Mother full of grace, I know
> You live in great poverty, wanting nothing more
> No raptures, no miracles, no ecstasies
> Adorn your life, O Queen of the Elect!
> The number of little ones on earth is very great
> They can raise their eyes to you without trembling
> It is the common path, incomparable Mother,
> You are pleased to tread so you can guide them to Heaven.[207]

In his poem *Regina Angelorum*, Chesterton makes the same observation:

> Our Lady went into a strange country,
> Our Lady, for she was ours,
> And had run on the little hills behind the houses
> And pulled small flowers;
> But she rose up and went into a strange country
> With strange thrones and powers ...

> Our Lady wears a crown in a strange country,
> The crown He gave,
> But she has not forgotten to call to her old companions
> To call and crave;
> And to hear her calling a man might arise and thunder
> On the doors of the grave.[208]

The Mother of God is truly *Our* Lady, really *ours*. In the fine sensitivity of her glorified body and God-seeing soul, she knows

---

[205] See Léthel, *Connaître*, pp. 502f.
[206] PN 54, 'Pourquoi je t'aime, ô Marie', OC 751.
[207] Ibid., 754.
[208] *Regina Angelorum*, Mackey, p. 157.

our every small need. She is Queen of Heaven, but she brings everything down to earth.

During her trial of faith, Thérèse walks confidently into the dark with her hand in Mary's. 'Mother, your sweet Child wants me to be an example / Of the soul that seeks Him in the night of faith.'[209] Hearing these verses of Thérèse, one thinks of some of Chesterton's, of his *Ballad of the White Horse*, for example, where Our Lady says that 'the men signed of the Cross of Christ / Go gaily in the dark'.[210] Thérèse is comforted not only by Our Lady's motherly prayers from Heaven, but also by the example of Our Lady's own trial of faith on Calvary. She realizes that the divine Bridegroom is giving her a small share in the co-redemptive night of His Mother.

> It was the will of the King of Heaven that His Mother
> Should be plunged into the night, into anguish of heart;
> Mary, does that mean it is good to suffer on earth?
> Yes, suffering in loving is the purest good fortune!
> All that He has given me Jesus can take back
> Tell Him never to bother about me ...
> He may hide Himself, I am ready to wait for Him
> Without resting till the day my faith is no more ...[211]

In Chesterton's darkest days, in the early 1890s, long before he would call himself an Anglo-Catholic or become a Roman Catholic, his mind turned to Our Lady. He was sure she would bring light to him as she had to men of other Dark Ages.

> And e'en as she walked as one dreaming, sweet,
>   pale as the evening star,
> The spell of the wanton was snapped, and the revel of the gods
>   rolled afar,
> And she brightened the glens that were gloomy, and softened
>   the tribes that were wild,
> Till the world grew a worshipping choir round the shapes of a
>   Mother and Child.

[209] PN 54, 'Pourquoi je t'aime, ô Marie', OC 753.
[210] Mackey, p. 216.
[211] Ibid., 754.

O woman, O maiden and mother, now also we need thee to greet:
Now in ages of change and question, I come with a prayer
                                                to thy feet,
In the earthquake and cleaving of strata, the lives of low
                                                passions we see,
And the horrors we bound in dark places rejoice, having hope
                                                to be free;
Wild voices from hills half-forgotten laugh scorn at all
                                                bonds that restrain:
O queen of all tender and holy, come down and confound them
        again![212]

The Little Way – Our Lady as Motherly Mediatrix

Our Lady *is* the Little Way. She is our Mother in the order of grace, the Mediatrix of All Graces. All the graces for a childlike life of Faith, Hope, and Charity come from the Heart of Jesus through the motherly intercession of Mary. Moreover, it is through true devotion to the Blessed Virgin, by entrusting ourselves to her as motherly Advocate, that we learn – in the Holy Spirit – to approach Jesus and the Father in the manner of children.

St Thérèse was deeply and gratefully aware of Our Lady's motherly mediation of grace in her life. On the Feast of Pentecost 1883[213] she was cured of a mysterious and debilitating illness through 'the ravishing smile of the Virgin'.[214] Later she began to doubt whether the Virgin truly did smile at her. This scruple disappeared in November 1887 in the church of Our Lady of Victories in Paris, just before the trip to Rome with her father.[215] Two years later, in July 1889, only a few months after her father's admission to the asylum, Thérèse received a second special gift from the Mother of God. While praying in a hermitage in the convent garden, she felt herself taken under the Virgin's mantle.[216]

---

[212] *Ave Maria*, printed in *The Debater*, Feb. 1893, Mackey, p. 112.

[213] It was 13 May, the date on which, thirty-four years later, Our Lady would appear at Fatima to the children.

[214] MS A, 30r, OC 117.

[215] Cf. MS A, 56v, OC 164.

[216] CJ, 11 July 1897, OC 1036.

The heavenly mission of the Mother of God is, by her prayers, to conform us to the childhood of her Son.

> I am looking [she says] for a child
> Like Jesus, my only Lamb,
> To keep them both together
> In the same cradle ...

> I will hide you beneath the veil
> Where shelters the King of Heaven,
> My Son will be the only star
> Henceforth shining in your eyes.

> But if I am to shelter you for ever
> Beneath my veil, close to Jesus,
> You will have to stay small,
> Adorned with childlike virtues ...[217]

Chesterton, too, knew that the mission of the Mother of God is to make us childlike in our approach to Jesus and the Father, children-in-the Child, sons-in-the-Son. In *Christendom in Dublin*, when describing the Irish Madonna he bought and presented to the church of St Thérèse in Beaconsfield, he told again a great story of the Irish people:

> She looks across the church with an intense earnestness in which there is something of endless youth; and I have sometimes started, as if I had actually heard the words spoken across that emptiness: *I am the Mother of God, and this is Himself, and he is the boy you will all be wanting at the last.*[218]

'Something of endless youth': in those words Chesterton makes his own the doctrine of Thérèse's countryman and contemporary, Charles Péguy, who said that the Mother of God is 'infinitely little' and 'infinitely young'.[219] Another Frenchman, Georges Bernanos, who was greatly devoted to St Thérèse, repeated the refrain: the Blessed Virgin is 'younger than sin'.[220] These two, like Thérèse and Gilbert, realized that in both soul

---

[217] PN 13, 'La Reine du Ciel à son enfant bien-aimée Marie de la Ste Face', OC 659f.

[218] *Christendom in Dublin* (London, 1932), pp. 71f.

[219] Porche, OPC 202.

[220] See pp. 117f. below.

and body Our Lady now enjoys in Heaven the eternal youth which her divine Son wants to give us all. By her Immaculate Conception, she is younger than sin. By her Assumption, she is younger than death.

God's Mother is our Mother – more Mother than Queen. It was not enough for Thérèse to call her 'Mother'. She called her *Maman*, 'Mummy', because it was more tender.[221] In the hideous torture of 23 August 1897 she cried out 'Ma petite Mère! ... Maman, maman, maman'.[222] As we have seen, by her Little Way, St Thérèse can help rekindle our devotion to the Fatherhood of God. She will also lead us to a more fervent devotion to the spiritual maternity of Mary. Writing to her sister Céline, she opens up the heart of her devotion to the Virgin.

> With regard to the Blessed Virgin, I must confide to you one of the little things I do with her. Sometimes I surprise myself by saying to her: 'My dear Blessed Virgin, I think that I am happier than you, because I have you for Mother, but you don't have the Blessed Virgin to love ... True, you are the Mother of Jesus, but Jesus has given us to you completely ... and on the Cross He gave you us as Mother. So we are richer than you, because we possess Jesus, and you are ours, too.[223]

Only a child could approach the Mother of God in this way, but then, this is the way, the little way, God and His Mother want us to take.

The Little Way of Mary is the road to victory in the Lamb. This is the argument of St Thérèse's play 'The Triumph of Humility', which dramatizes Satan's campaign of hatred against the Church and her religious. He has a simple tactic: get the nuns to be absorbed with themselves, in imitation of his own narcissistic pride. He has some weighing-scales, on one side of which he places three scrolls representing the Vows of Religion. On the other side, he adds three scrolls bearing the inscriptions, 'Pride, Independence, Self-Will'. The Vows are outweighed. But then St Michael appears with a small scroll with only one word

---

[221] MS A, 57r, OC 164.
[222] CJ, 23 August 1897, 1107.
[223] LT 137, 19 October 1892, to Céline, OC 452.

on it: 'Humility.' When added to the Vows, it easily outweighs the scrolls of demonic egoism. The good archangel addresses the evil one:

> I want to prove your folly to you again.
> Do you forget, serpent, infernal monster,
> *The humility of the Virgin Mary*
> Who crushed you with her virginal foot?

Lucifer shrieks with despair: 'I am defeated ... I am defeated!'[224] The littleness of the Immaculate Heart has triumphed, as it always will.

5. *Look for Them in the Nurseries of Heaven*

The saints bring the light of the risen Christ to the darkest of dark ages. The mission of St Thérèse, above as it was here below, was to be a dawn of Christian hope for the nihilistic night of her own century and ours. In this life we cannot know how much the great converts of the late Victorian and Edwardian age owed to the merits of her tested faith on earth and to the intercessions of her triumphant vision in Heaven.[225] Such is the mystery of the *communio sanctorum*. Charles Péguy, the Revolutionary Socialist, became a Catholic of the Catechism and Pilgrim of Our Lady. Oscar Wilde died a Catholic in 1900, fortified by the rites of the Church. His fellow Decadent, Aubrey Beardsley, converted in the very year of Thérèse's death. 'It is such a rest,' he said, 'to be folded after all my wanderings.'[226] Most astonishing of all was the conversion of Ernest Psichari, the grandson of Ernest Renan. He was received into the Church in 1913 and died as a hero of France, with a rosary wrapped round his wrist, in the first days of the First World War. When he was being

[224] RP 7, 'Le Triomphe de l'Humilité', OC 925.

[225] According to Catholic doctrine, the justified man *de congruo* (by the merit of fittingness) can merit for other people the first actual grace of justification. 'Since a man in the state of grace fulfils the will of God, it is fitting, in harmony with friendship, that God should fulfil the will of that man in regard to the salvation of another person, even though there may sometimes be an impediment on the part of the man whose justification the holy man desires' (St Thomas Aquinas, *Summa theologiae*, 1a2ae 114, 6).

[226] See Holbrook Jackson, *The Eighteen Nineties*, p. 31.

instructed, he was comforted by the suggestion of a priest that 'the soul of Renan, at the moment it appeared before God, might perhaps have been relieved of its faults through the prayer of some Carmelite, through the tears of some very humble contemplative'.[227]

Chesterton's conversion took place one year before the beatification of Thérèse, the humble Carmelite contemplative. Though she is seldom mentioned by him in his writings, she was destined to play a not insignificant role in his life. On his last visit to France, only weeks before his death, Gilbert visited Lisieux, and he is buried within a parish whose church is dedicated to the Little Flower and built in part out of his benefaction. In one of his last letters, written from Lourdes, he revealed that he was beginning to 'honour and understand [her] better'.[228] Today, if the purgation of his soul has been completed (and he would not want us to presume it had been), Gilbert and Thérèse are children together and for ever, playing with the Child Jesus in the park that is Paradise. In Heaven, as once on earth, theirs is the Little Way. Each of them speaks to us now in the words of another of their Catholic contemporaries, a man whom Chesterton numbered among the great poets of our tongue,[229] Francis Thompson:

> Pass where majestical the eternal peers,
> The stately choice of the great Saintdom, meet –
> A silvern segregation, globed complete
> In sandalled shadow of the Triune feet ...
> Pass the crystalline sea, the Lampads seven –
> Look for me in the nurseries of Heaven.[230]

---

[227] Henri Massis, *La vie de Ernest Psichari* (Paris, 1920), pp. 42f.

[228] Ward, *Return*, pp. 268f.

[229] Of Thompson's 'Hound of Heaven', Chesterton said that it was 'the greatest religious poem of modern times and one of the greatest of all times' (*The Common Man* [New York, 1950], p. 132).

[230] Francis Thompson, 'To My Godchild', *Collected Poems* (London, 1913), p. 16.

2

Charles Péguy and the Victory of the Innocents

Péguy is mentioned only once in the works of Chesterton, but it is an honourable mention, a kind of citation for bravery. In an essay on Rostand, Chesterton praises the part played by Péguy and Claudel in 'the process which banished the birds of barbaric night from the land of the Eagles of the sun'.[1] The night was the nihilism of the Nineties, the 'pessimism' that, in France as in England, was 'the shadow of Prussianism', the gloom of Wagner in music and of Schopenhauer and Nietzsche in philosophy. Péguy would have been pleased with the tribute. His life was a battle of hope against despair, and his soldierly death in 1914 was in the defence of France against the Prussian *Übermensch* and the desperate 'will to power'.

It is good to know that Chesterton admired Péguy, sad that he said so little about him, for Péguy was a paradox so vast that only a Chestertonian girth of mind can comprehend it. He was a revolutionary, but the revolution that he proposed was moral, not political. He wanted to be a simple parish Catholic, true to the faith which he lost, but then recovered,[2] and yet, having married outside the Church, he was unable to receive the Sacraments, and his children were not baptized until after his death. He marched to Chartres as a pilgrim of

---

[1] *The Uses of Diversity*, p. 105.
[2] In September 1908 he told a friend: 'I have found my faith again. I am a Catholic' (OPC xxxviii). He lost his faith because he could not accept the doctrine of eternal punishment.

Our Lady, but on arrival, he halted on the cathedral steps, not daring to enter. The posture is revealing. Péguy appears to be both inside and outside the Church; as Balthasar says, in his very person he is 'the Church *in partibus infidelium*, the Church in those places where the Church will be one day'.[3]

Although Péguy eludes capture by our categories, he should not be condemned to exile in complexity; nothing would have embarrassed him more. He hated self-conscious cleverness with a perfect hatred: 'scientificism' and 'artistry', he said, are the very 'arms of Satan'.[4] The aim of his art was to subvert the pretentious 'systems' of ideology that befog the mind of man. In poetry and politics, above all in religion, he prized simplicity. He was convinced that men and women best serve truth, goodness, and beauty when they convert and become like little children.[5] There is a revolutionary power in innocence, he says, and only there. It is the spotless Lamb that overcomes the world, the Immaculate Heart that triumphs. Charles Péguy is not only the contemporary of St Thérèse and Gilbert Chesterton, but their comrade in arms. Together they fight for God against the child-devouring Dragon. Péguy deploys militant prose and meditative poetry to expound, in the 'lay style',[6] a Catholic theology of childhood. In this chapter I shall sketch its chief features. It is an outline of sanity for a world that is insanely slaying its young.

First is Fairest

We must begin at the beginning, always a good place to start. Péguy wanted to keep faith with the 'initial purities' of his life: the waters of his baptism, the answers of his catechism, his childhood games by a Catholic hearth, the soil of his father-

---

[3] Hans Urs von Balthasar, *Herrlichkeit. Eine theologische Ästhetik*, Band 2, Fächer der Stile, Teil 2, Laikale Stile (Einsiedeln, 1962), p. 772.

[4] Geneviève, OPC 850. See also *L'esprit de système*, new edition (Paris, 1953), and Dejond, pp. 81f.

[5] His own verse has the repetitions of a song of the playground.

[6] Balthasar, op. cit., includes Péguy as an example of the 'lay style' of 'theological aesthetic'.

land.[7] What comes first is fairest. Beginnings are beautiful, for at the start everything is intact and unspoilt.

> All that is small is the loveliest and greatest of all,
> All that is young is the loveliest and greatest of all,
> Baptism is the sacrament of little ones,
> Baptism is the youngest sacrament of all,
> Baptism is the beginning sacrament,
> Anything that has a beginning has a power it never recovers,
> A force, a newness, a freshness like the dawn,
> A youthfulness, an ardour,
> An enthusiasm,
> A naïveté,
> A birth it never regains,
> The first day is the loveliest day of all,
> The first day is perhaps the only lovely day,
> And Baptism is the sacrament of the first day,
> And Baptism is the loveliest and greatest of all,
> Were it not for the Sacrifice,
> And the eating of the Body of Our Lord.[8]

Péguy is a down-to-earth thinker. When he speaks of 'little ones', he is thinking of the actual boy he used to be and of his own three children, 'who at this very moment are playing by the fireside'.[9] He presents childhood as a wellspring of renewal, because, in the mid-course of his life, he has felt its rejuvenating power. Through his children this man has become young again. *Heureux enfants, heureux père.*[10]

> In the child, in childhood, there is a unique grace,
> A wholeness, a firstness
> Something total,

[7] 'He received first of all the gift of fidelity: a profound attachment to these initial purities, and to all purity. And it is because he confronts the existence of peoples, of men, his own existence, with this absolute purity that he feels the anguish of aging, the condemnation inflicted by time on all that is of time' (Béguin, *Prière*, p. 17).

[8] Porche, OPC 550.

[9] Ibid., 556. 'For Péguy, layman and father of a family, family life is the essential place of Christian life, of all Christian life, of life in Christ' (Léthel, *Connaître*, p. 378).

[10] Porche, OPC 553.

An origin, a secret, source, a point of origin,
An as it were absolute beginning,
Children are new creatures.[11]

Péguy does not forget that natural childhood's 'force' and
'freshness' can be spoilt and wasted by adult wickedness, that
its chronological 'firstness' will never be regained. His catechism taught him that no fallen child of Adam is innocent as
Jesus and Mary were innocent. And yet he also knew that a
newborn baby, though born in Original Sin, is wholly free from
actual sin, and that, once re-born in Baptism, is blessed with the
supernatural innocence of an adopted son of God. Baptism is
the 'sacrament of little ones', the 'youngest sacrament of all',
not just because it is administered to babies, but because, even
when conferred on adults, it makes men babies. As both the
Fathers and the liturgy teach us, the newly baptized, whatever
their calendrical age, are *infantes*, newborn of God. 'They went
in as old men', says St Augustine, 'they came out as infants.'[12]
These are the facts of human and Christian existence, and for
Péguy, they were fixed points of reference, bright pole-stars, for
the future navigation of life.

The Richness of Innocence

Péguy the Catholic, like Péguy the Socialist, was a revolutionary. He wanted to subvert, not a mere system of govern-
ment, but a whole state of mind, the characteristic outlook of

---

[11] Innocents, OPC 788.

[12] *Tractatus 1 in epistolam Ioannis ad Parthos*, n. 5; PL 45. 1982. St Augustine's
sermons addressed to neophytes are *sermones ad infantes* (cf. *Sermones* 224–
228, *Ad infantes*; PL 38. 1093ff.). In the Blessing of the Font at the Easter Vigil,
as Péguy would have remembered it from his boyhood, the Church prays
that the man there baptized be 're-born into a new infancy of true innocence'. On Low Sunday, *Dominica in albis*, when the new Christians are
still wearing the white robes of their baptism, the Church sings an introit
from St Peter's First Epistle: *Quasi modo geniti infantes* ... 'As newborn
babes, desire the rational milk without guile, that thereby you may grow
unto salvation' (1 Pet. 2:2). 'Know you what it is to be a child?' asked
Francis Thompson, 'It is to have a spirit yet streaming from the waters
of Baptism' ('Shelley', *The Works of Francis Thompson*, vol. 3 [London, n.d.],
p. 7).

the 'modern world': 'laicist, positivist, and atheistic'.[13] In his journalism, as in his verse, he asked his readers not to suspend their doubt but to re-direct it towards the dogmas of worldly wisdom and in particular towards the slavish devotion of the present age to *experience*. He rebelled against the tyranny of the 'man of the world', who has 'seen it all' and lost his capacity for wonder.

> They say they're full of experience; they gain from
>   experience.
> They learn about life; day by day they pile up their
>   experience.
> Some treasure, says God.
> A treasury of emptiness and of dearth ...
> A treasury of wrinkles and worries.
> The treasure of the lean years ...
> What you call experience, your experience, I call
>   dissipation, diminution, decrease, the loss of
>   innocence.
> It's a perpetual degradation.
> No, it is innocence which is full and experience which
>   is empty.
> It is innocence which wins and experience which
>   loses.
> It is innocence which is young and experience which
>   is old.
> It is innocence which increases and experience
>   which decreases.
> It is innocence which is born and experience which
>   dies.
> It is innocence which knows and experience which
>   does not know.
> It is the child who is full and it is the man who is
>   empty.
> Like an empty gourd, like an empty beer-barrel.

[13] Cf. 'Zangwill', OPR 1, 683. 'The struggle is not between one world and another. The struggle is between all other worlds together and the modern world. All other worlds (except the modern world) have been worlds of some kind of spirituality. Only the modern world, as the world of money, is the world of a total and absolute materiality' ('Note conjointe sur M. Descartes', OPR 2, 1535).

So then, says God, that's what I think of your
experience.[14]

Charles Péguy did not condemn the aging process, nor did
he canonize childishness. He simply refused to accept that a
child's losing of his innocence was the prerequisite for his
attainment of maturity. Péguy's mission was a struggle to death
against 'the pretentious loss, the diminution, the waning, the
waste of hope'.[15] He shared Chesterton's suspicion that the truly
grown-up person, the man in full enjoyment of his maturity,
'recalls with secret predilection the age of innocence'.[16] He was
haunted by the fall from innocence not just of the individual
but of the whole race of man. In our First Parents, we were all
expelled from Paradise. The sons of Adam are born deprived of
that Original Justice which was a primeval innocence.[17] Like
Chesterton, Péguy finds this dogma – the dogma of Original
Sin – not only enlightening but encouraging, because it teaches
the human heart that 'happiness is not only a hope but also in
some strange manner a memory'.[18] In this perspective, at once
Patristic and Péguyesque, redemption is achieved by recapitu-
lation, through a new beginning that includes the old, through

[14] Innocents, OPC 787. Cardinal Newman makes a similar critique of
experience: 'They think it manly to taste the pleasures of sin, they think it
manly to know what sin is before condemning it . . . They look down upon the
innocent, upon women and children, and solitaries, and holy and humble men
of heart, who, like the Cherubim, see God and worship, as unfit for the great
business of life, and worthless in the real estimate of things' ('The State of
Innocence', *Parochial and Plain Sermons*, vol. 5, new edition [London, 1878], p.
110).

[15] Ibid.

[16] 'Notes pour une thèse', OPR 2, 1177. In his *Autobiography*, Chesterton said
that among the many books he had not written was a novel about 'a successful
city man who seemed to have a dark secret in his life; and who was eventually
discovered by the detectives still playing with dolls or tin soldiers or some
undignified antic of infancy' (pp. 44f.).

[17] This is well discussed by Albert Béguin in *L'Ève de Péguy* (Paris, 1948),
passim.

[18] *GK's Weekly* (25 September 1926). Newman, speaking of the state of
Original Innocence, says: 'In the past we see the future as if in miniature and
outline' ('The State of Innocence', *Parochial and Plain Sermons*, vol. 5, p. 100).
Thus 'in aiming to be children again, we are aiming to be as Adam on his
creation' (ibid., p. 102).

the regaining of Paradise, the coming of a New Adam and New Eve who embrace and retrieve the Old. This is a revolutionary insight. It runs counter to the Victorian cult of Progress, indeed to every post-Enlightenment myth of a world come of age. Truth and goodness are not determined by the ticking of the clock. In Christianity, says Péguy, there is 'no progress of any kind. Only modern men make progress. But we are ... no cleverer than St. John Chrysostom'.[19] This is not whimsy but exact orthodoxy. The development of doctrine is not the invention of novelties but the unfolding of a treasure ever ancient, ever new, the immortal diamond of Divine Revelation, the faith once delivered to the saints. The pilgrim Church, however far into history she walks, never outpaces the Apostles, from whom, through the Fathers, she received her faith. As an early Christian visionary perceived, the Church is a woman at once old and young, old because all the righteous from Abel are her children, young because she is alive with the life of the risen Christ.[20]

During Péguy's lifetime, that innocence of faith which the Church calls orthodoxy was violated by Modernism. Péguy abhorred 'the Modernist superstition'. He defined it as 'not believing what one believes'. The Modernists were guilty of theological humbug, what Bernanos would later call *imposture*,[21] an adult duplicity that is the opposite of childhood's simplicity. The Modernist cleric lives a lie: he enjoys the social advantages of priesthood while undermining the dogmatic faith that alone gives the priesthood its meaning. Péguy tears down the romanticized picture of the heretic as a brave defender of intellectual liberty. Modernism is 'a system of cowardice', a craven capitulation to everything that crushes true freedom: the 'determinism and materialism and associationism' of the *monde moderne*.[22] Theological dissent is the plaything of the self-indulgent, 'the virtue of the top people'.[23]

[19] Laudet, OPR 2, 918.
[20] Cf. *The Shepherd of Hermas*, vision 2, n. 4; J. B. Lightfoot, ed., *The Apostolic Fathers* (London, 1907), p. 302.
[21] See pp. 103f. below.
[22] 'Note conjointe sur M. Descartes', OPR 2, 1510.
[23] 'L'Argent', OPR 2, 1136.

Péguy foresaw that the 'liberal' theologians, far from liberating man, would end up endorsing the modern world's programmes for his enslavement. The most flagrant example in his lifetime was that of the apostate Ernest Renan, whose 'humanist' rejection of Christ led to an anti-human adulation of science. For Renan, as for a whole faithless generation in France and England, the conviction that the human race was capable of deifying itself through scientific advance was 'viaticum, consolation, hope, secret ardour, interior fire, laicist eucharist'. With what Balthasar has called 'metaphysical horror', Péguy denounced Renan's eugenical dream of a brave new world inhabited by 'a superior race', 'a species of gods and goddesses', beings who would use man as he now uses animals.[24] The lesson of the Renan story is plain: it is God's 'daughter', the Catholic Church, the humble Church of the parish, that defends man, from conception to the last breath, while proud Modernism is a recipe for his abolition.

The Youthfulness of the Eternal Trinity

Childhood and youth, according to Péguy, reflect something of the eternity of the Triune God. For Catholic orthodoxy, there is no time or succession in Him Who Is. He exists in an eternal present, without shift from the past or lurch to the future. He possesses His boundless life wholly, simultaneously, and perfectly.[25] Péguy had an intuition that, while God is indeed 'the Ancient of Days', the divine eternity and vitality are best expressed by the imagery of youth. The everlasting God is not so much exceedingly old as immeasurably young.[26] Age does not weary Him, nor do the years condemn:

---

[24] 'Zangwill', OPR 1, 707ff. On Péguy's view of Renan, see Balthasar, op. cit., p. 780, and Dejond, pp. 31f.

[25] Cf. Boethius, *De consolatione philosophiae* 5, 6; and St Thomas Aquinas, *Summa theologiae*, 1a 10, 1.

[26] Newman has the same insight: 'What shall we say of the Eternal God but that He, *because* He is eternal, is ever *young*, without a beginning, and therefore without change, and, in the fulness and perfection of His incomprehensible attributes, now just what He was a million years ago? He is truly called in Scripture the "Ancient of Days", and is therefore infinitely venerable, yet he

And God Himself young and eternal
Looked at the games being played by the young.
Calmly His fatherly eyes rested on man
And in him He considered His own image ...
And God Himself young and eternal
Looked at what children are like at their first stage ...

And God Himself young and eternal
Looked at what young lads are like.
As Father He cast His fatherly eyes
On a mother bending over two cradles.[27]

In the Godhead, the Father eternally begets the Son, and the Son is eternally begotten of the Father. Thus, by the strict logic of the Nicene Creed, the Son is as 'old' as the Father, and the Father as 'young' as the Son. In medieval images of the Trinity, God the Father often appears as a Christ-like youth, and fittingly so, for the eternal Son is the consubstantial Image of the Father and in His resurrected human body is ever young. I believe that Péguy glimpsed these high peaks of dogma, not after years of theological toil, but through the charisms of prophecy and poetry vouchsafed him in his final years.

The Child-God

The believing Péguy is before all else a doctor of the Incarnation.[28] Albert Béguin compares his Christ-centredness to that of Pascal:

For Pascal, 'Jesus Christ is at the centre of everything,' the key to the mystery of God, but also the key to man, and the key to natural creation. Similarly, for Péguy, *Et Verbum caro factum est* is

---

needs not old age to make Him venerable' ('Meditations on the Litany of Loretto for the Month of May', *Prayers, Verses, and Devotions* [San Francisco, 1989], p. 130).

[27] Ève, OPC 1061ff. The Romantic poets recalled childhood as a brief time that seemed to have the length of eternity: 'Sweet childish days', says Wordsworth, 'that were as long / As twenty days are now' ('To a Butterfly', *The Poetical Works of Wordsworth* [London, 1904], p. 106).

[28] 'In Péguy's theology, as in that of St Anselm, the expression *Deus homo*, "the God-Man", is absolutely central' (Léthel, *Connaître*, p. 377).

the centre around which everything is organized and becomes intelligible.[29]

The things of earth and of the body are good and beautiful because they have been created by the infinitely good and beautiful God, and when God is made flesh in the Virgin's womb, they are exalted, at least objectively, to a matchless dignity and an imperishable destiny:

> For the supernatural is itself carnal
> And the tree of grace is rooted deep
> And plunges into the soil and reaches right down
> And the tree of the race is itself eternal ...
> And Jesus is the fruit of a Mother's womb ...[30]

In *Ève*, Péguy gazes at the Child-God in the manger, sleeping at peace in the depths of materiality and history, the neighbour of ox and ass and the heir of the Old Testament and all the wisdom of pagan Egypt, Greece, and Rome. The whole order of space and time, in all its richness and complexity, is recapitulated and renewed in this baby in the hay, the infant Creator Word.

> He was going to inherit a world already made
> And yet He was going to re-make it whole and entire.
> He was going to overflow from cause to effect
> As a river overflows and spreads to new land.[31]

In the womb of His Mother, God the Son took the way of childhood into the world, and thus united Himself to every child, made all the *parvuli* His brethren and playmates. Of all children, therefore, we can say that they are 'sweet children, inimitable children, Jesus' brothers'.[32] In a certain sense, says Péguy, through the Incarnation, all children *are* the child Jesus: *Vous êtes tous des enfants Jesus.*

> You children imitate Jesus.
> No, you don't imitate Him. You *are* Child-Jesuses ...

[29] Béguin, *L'Ève de Péguy* (Paris, 1948), p. 25.
[30] Ève, OPC 1041, 1043.
[31] Ibid., 1087.
[32] Porche, OPC 553.

Man, any man, the greatest saint, any saint knows
    he's infinitely far from Jesus.
In his imitation.
Irreparable loss, descent, fall, inevitable wasting away
    of life.
Such is existence, life, aging.
In our childhood we are joined to Jesus.
As we grow up we are disjoined from Him,
    we disjoin ourselves
from Him our whole life long.
You are hopes as the Child Jesus was a hope.
You really are Child-Jesuses.[33]

With these bold words, Péguy draws some reasonable conclusions from the doctrine of Christ's Headship as expounded by St Paul, St Irenaeus, St Augustine, and St Thomas Aquinas. Though not every man is joined to Christ the Head by Baptism, Christ the Head is somehow joined to every man by the Incarnation.[34] As man, but because He is God, the Son sums up all mankind, all creation, in Himself (cf. Eph. 1:10). That is why when any man is served or neglected, it is Christ in him who is served or neglected. 'Truly, I say to you, as you did it to one of the least of these my brethren, you did it to me' (Matt. 25:40). Children are indeed the 'least' of Christ's brethren, the smallest and most vulnerable of His kinsmen. Their childhood is the first state of human life that the Son of God made His own. He could have created for Himself, as He did for Adam, a human nature in adult form,[35] but instead, freely and lovingly, He took the

---

[33] Ibid., 554.

[34] See the Second Vatican Council's Pastoral Constitution on the Church in the Modern World, *Gaudium et spes*, n. 22. This does not imply that the Incarnation 'automatically' confers salvation on the whole human race. While the Son of God, in becoming incarnate, has joined Himself to every man, every man, every son of Adam affected by his sin, must still be joined to Him, incorporated as an individual member of His Mystical Body.

[35] St Thomas cites the authority of St Augustine on this question: 'God could have assumed human nature from some other source, and not from the race of that Adam who by his sin enthralled the human race, but He judged it better to take up human nature from that conquered race, and through human nature to conquer the enemy of the human race' (*Summa theologiae*, 3a 4, 6; cf. St Augustine, *De Trinitate*, 13, 18, 23; CCSL 50A. 413).

little and lowly way into human life, the path that led Him to be conceived by the Holy Spirit and born of the Virgin Mary, 'made of a woman' (Gal. 4:4). Children have a special affinity with Christ. The Babe of Bethlehem awaits our veneration in every womb and in every cradle.

In seeing the Child Jesus in all the babies of the world, we are participating by faith in the vision of God the Father, for in the Holy Innocents of Bethlehem, in every human child, He finds a reflection of His beloved consubstantial Son. The gaze of the 'young and eternal God' is kindly. His words are homely. As Julien Green has said, Péguy makes the First Person of the Trinity sound 'like an elderly French peasant well versed in his catechism'.[36]

> They were like my Son
> And He was like them ...
> My Son was tender like them, and like them He was new,
> He was as unknown. As them ...
> [T]hey remind me of my Son.
> As if He hadn't changed since then, when He was so beautiful.
> As if this vast adventure
> Had stopped there. That is why I love them, says God,
>   above all they are the *witnesses* of my Son.
> They show me, they are as He was, if only He hadn't changed.
> Of all the imitations of Jesus Christ
> This is the first and this is the freshest. It is the only one
> That is not to any degree
> That is not even to the slightest extent
> An imitation of any kind of blot or bruise or wound on the soul
>   of Jesus.
> It is a total ignorance of insult or disgrace.
> Of injury and offence ...
> For me they are children who have never become men,
> Lambs who never became rams,
> Nor ewes. (*And these follow the Lamb wherever He goes*).
> Child Jesuses who will never grow old. Who will never
>   grow.
> *Now my Son advanced in wisdom and in age, and in grace*
>   *with God and with men.*

[36] Julien Green, *Charles Péguy: Basic Verities* (London, 1943), p. 333.

They are the eternal imitations
Of what Jesus was for a very short time
For He *increased*. He grew
For the sake of this enormous adventure.
And the seventh reason, says God, is that they are just as
   David wanted them to be,
Immaculati in via.[37]

Charles Péguy recognized, as did St Paul, that the day comes for every man when he must put away 'the things of a child' (cf. 1 Cor. 13:11). Such renunciation is natural and normal, and, as St Thérèse learnt, the natural presupposition for the supernatural graces of spiritual childhood.[38] There is no one less childlike than the man who with adult obstinacy refuses to grow up. However, because of the abiding wounds in our fallen humanity, the natural leaving of childhood is often a violent sundering. The world and its prince tempt man to exchange childhood's simplicity for the pride of life, to cast into oblivion those first years of weakness and dependence. By contrast, the God-Man, the New Adam, though He advanced into adulthood (cf. Luke 2:52), never retreated from His childhood. His human life on earth, from the Virgin's womb to the Easter tomb, was an untorn tapestry of humility and obedience to the Father. Even on Golgotha, says Madame Gervaise to St Joan, Jesus thought of Bethlehem. He saw life's beginning in its end, its end in its beginning.

> Life begun in Bethlehem and ended in Jerusalem.
> Life contained between Bethlehem and Jerusalem.
> Life inscribed between Bethlehem and Jerusalem.
> He saw again the humble cradle of His childhood ...
> The crib where His body was first laid down;
> He foresaw the great tomb of His dead body,
> The last cradle of every man,
> Where every man has to lie down.[39]

---

[37] Innocents, OPC 817ff.

[38] See pp. 37f. above.

[39] Mystère, OPC 437. There is a beautiful example of the unity of the mysteries of the life of Jesus, of Bethlehem with Calvary, in the life of the medieval English hermit, St Godric of Finchale (1065–1170). The saint had a vision of the Christ Child appearing from out of the wounded side (and thus

Péguy denounced the campaign of Modernist theology (based on the scepticism of Modernist exegesis) to remove the so-called 'infancy narratives' from the Gospels and focus exclusively on the adult doings of the Public Ministry and Passion. In an article written in 1911, he replied to the argument of Fernand Laudet (in the latter's critique of *The Mystery of the Charity of Joan of Arc*) that the Maid of Orléans belongs to us as missionary and martyr but not as young girl, 'just as Christ only belongs to us from the day it pleased Him to leave the years of dense shadow'. Péguy fired back a broadside: 'Monsieur Laudet will do well not to despise too much the Joan of Arc of "when we were small". Nor perhaps the Jesus Christ of "when we were small".'[40] What Laudet is doing, suggests Péguy, is robbing the God-Man of His childhood and Jewish family life, cutting Him off from His hidden years of play and prayer and labour:

> In the system, in the theology of Monsieur Laudet, all the patience, in work, in existence itself, all the work, this whole life of work, of obedience and of humiliation which Jesus offered to His Father right up to the beginning of His thirtieth year doesn't enter into the Communion of Saints, is not a life of merit; it is a life which does not count.[41]

Péguy perceived that a Christology without Christmas, a Sermon on the Mount without the Son in the Manger, produces a falsely 'adult' religion, a species of Adoptionism, according to which Christ is a mere man who has 'grown up' into divinity, an enlightened teacher and moral example, another Buddha or Socrates. This was not a Christ for whom a man might die, whether in the sand of the Colosseum or in the fields of Flanders. The Christ of Péguy was the Christ of 'when we were small', the Catholic Christ of the Catechism, the great God

---

heart) of an image of the Crucified. St Godric cried out: 'Good Jesus, sweet Jesus, merciful and most kind Jesus, have pity on me a miserable little man!' (see the splendid work by my friend, the late Father Francis Rice, *The Hermit of Finchale. The Life of St Godric* (Edinburgh, 1994), pp. 131f.).

[40] Laudet, OPR 2, 902.
[41] Ibid., 909.

incarnate, the eternal Son, who, without ceasing to be true God, was made true man in the Virgin's womb, to save poor Adam and his stock from sin and death and the power of Satan. This is the only true Jesus. Here is no Prometheus but the strong and childlike God-Man who even in the Garden prays 'Abba, Father'.[42] 'Jesus belongs to us whole and entire', sings Péguy in unison with the saints: the one Christ in His divinity and humanity; the unique Saviour from Nazareth to Jerusalem; the only Son at the Father's right hand, in the womb of the Virgin, and in the tabernacles of the Church.

Reverence for the Innocent

The man who believes in Christmas, in the Child of the Virgin, has the greatest possible reason for revering childhood, for, as the whole work of Péguy bears witness, it was our true human childhood that the Son of God assumed and thus exalted. No man should forget the time 'when he was small', because there was a time when God Himself, as man, was small. When seen in the light of Bethlehem, childhood has much to teach the adult. The child, the boy I used to be or my own son at my knee, is a kind of icon of Christmas, a silent preaching of the *kenôsis*. Of such is the Kingdom of Heaven. Such is the King of Heaven.

If Péguy saw childhood in the light of the Word made flesh, he looked on the Word made flesh with the eyes of his childhood. As Albert Béguin has written:

> [Péguy] also owes to his childhood his respect for the earthly and the fleshly, which was to lead him to centre his world view on the fact of the Incarnation. The reason he affirmed the presence of the spiritual in lowly earthly realities was that he had been initiated into the spiritual as medieval believers were: by the concrete language of rites and images, and above all by the actions, the behaviour, the everyday conduct of the long Christianized people around him. This is why he mistrusts the 'letter', any kind of

---

[42] As did Bernanos after him, Péguy had an intense devotion to the mystery of Gethsemane. In 'Véronique' he compares and contrasts, in the manner of the Fathers, the *fiat lux* of Genesis and the *fiat voluntas tua* of the Garden, where we behold 'a God prostrate on the face of the earth' (OPR 2, 475).

abstraction, and why he is convinced that the simple soul is
blessed with a more direct closeness to the Spirit. This, too, is why
he loves the parish, the easily understandable, down-to-earth
form of Christianity: 'I am a parish man.'[43]

The Gospel of the Child

Péguy's sense of the ravages of time is reminiscent of the widespread late Victorian nostalgia for childhood's 'blue remembered hills'.[44] The difference is that Péguy, unlike an A. E.
Housman, accepts the fact and flow of time because he sees it
as a gift of the provident God who is at once 'eternal and
young'. When Péguy looks back at the child he used to be, he
reacts not with despair and remorse, but with penitence and
hope. We cannot re-enter our mother's wombs to resume our
physical infancy, but we can pray that the spiritual infancy of
our Baptism take hold of our lives and transform us. Through
the eternal Son, who for us became a human child, we can all
become children, again and for ever, as adopted sons of His
Father. It was for the sake of this re-birth of man in water and
the Spirit that the Father's Son was once born in the flesh. God
became a baby to make a sin-aged world young again in grace.[45]
As Péguy puts it, He came 'in the tired old fields to create a new
rye'.[46] Or, in the words he would have heard in church on
Christmas Day: 'May the new birth of thine Only-Begotten Son
in the flesh deliver us whom an old servitude holds fast beneath

[43] Béguin, Prière, p. 17.

[44] 'Into my heart an air that kills / From yon far country blows: / What are
those blue remembered hills, / What spires, what farms are those? / That is
the land of lost content, / I see it shining plain, / The happy highways where I
went / And cannot come again' (A. E. Housman, *A Shropshire Lad*, new edition
[London, 1922], p. 61).

[45] The eternal Word is conceived of a Virgin without male seed and born of
her without corruption, in a new modality of generation, because He comes to
makes all things new: 'If He had not summoned human oldness to a new
beginning by His birth, death would have reigned from Adam to the end'
(Pope St Leo the Great, *In nativitate Domini sermo V*, 5; SC 22B. 132).

[46] Ève, OPC 1065. 'In Jesus the world's movement towards nothingness and
death is arrested, brought to a standstill, and turned in its right and proper
direction' (Balthasar, op. cit., p. 485).

the yoke of sin.' The First Adam enslaves and makes old. The Second Adam sets free and makes new.

The Lord Jesus tells us that we cannot enter the Kingdom of Heaven unless we become like little children. This is the word and pledge, says Péguy, of God-made-man, and it is re-echoed in the teaching and 'Roman liturgy' of His Church. Péguy lets us hear God the Father's voice:

> My Son told them often enough.
> Without evasion and without attenuation.
> For He spoke plainly and firmly,
> And clearly.
> Blessed not only, not even,
> Is he who would be like a child, who would remain like a child.
> No, really blessed is he who is a child, who remains a child.
> Really, precisely the very child he has been.
> Because this is exactly what every man has been given.
> Because to every man it has been given to be
> A milky babe.
> Because to every man this blessing,
> This unique grace, has been given.[47]

We have not always been grim professors in grey suits. Once we were 'milky babes'. To recall our former helplessness with thankfulness is the first step towards the Kingdom of Heaven. Of course, the gift of natural childhood is lost through growing up, and the grace of supernatural adoption departs through mortal sin. However, the character of Baptism remains stamped upon our souls, and, by the rejuvenating Spirit of sonship, we can live in the truth of that character, as humble sons-in-the-Son of the Father. There is no need for remorse, says Péguy. While there is still breath in our body, we can always 'begin again'. The whole sacramental system of the Church is about fresh starts. Baptism is a new beginning in Christ, a second birth after our first birth into the oldness of Original Sin.[48] Penance is

[47] Innocents, OPC 785f.

[48] 'The origin that He had in the womb of the Virgin He placed within the font of Baptism. He gave to water what He gave to His Mother: the power of the Most High and the overshadowing of the Holy Spirit' (Pope St Leo the Great, *In nativitate Domini sermo V*, 5; SC 22B. 132).

a return to innocence after actual sin.[49] And the Sacrament of Sacraments, Holy Mass, is a re-commencement, a daily mystery of re-presentation, the sacramental renewal of the Sacrifice of Christ on Calvary. As Péguy reminds Fernand Laudet:

> This really is the life of Christendom. Prayer, sir, begins again all the time, the Sacrament begins again all the time. Birth itself and temporal death begin again all the time ... Temptation, unfortunately sin begins again all the time. All the time, every day, prayer begins again to ask God for each day's bread. The Sacrifice of the Mass all the time begins again the Sacrifice of the Cross.[50]

The Pedagogy of Péguy

This Catholic theology of childhood contains a Christian philosophy of education. If the mysteries of God's Kingdom are revealed to mere babes (cf. Matt. 11:25), if the whole of Christian life is about beginning again, then, so argues Péguy, Christian teachers must zealously guard the innocence of their children – their purity and wonder, their receptivity and zest for life. The protection of innocence is a religious duty, because the 'innocence of children is God's greatest glory'.[51] Sadly, in the modern world the school has become an apparatus for snuffing out bright innocence. Where Gradgrind is Headmaster, learning is dis-education. If wisdom is to be won, the un-learning must itself be un-learnt:

> They have schools, says God, I think they're for
> Un-learning
> The little they know.
> Go, my children, go to school,
> And you, men, go to the school of life,
> Go to learn
> To unlearn.[52]

---

[49] St Augustine says of penance: 'God can remove guilt and call a man back to innocence' (St Augustine, *Opus imperfectum contra Iulianum*, lib. 6; PL 45. 1544).

[50] Laudet, OPR 2, 980.

[51] Mystère, OPC 395.

[52] Innocents, OPC 786f.

The child can teach his teacher, especially in matters of prayer. Against the tendency to rigidify the stages of the spiritual life ('beginners', 'proficients', and the like) into ranks and regiments, Péguy, like St Thérèse, presents the pre-kindergarten child as the exemplary Christian pray-er:

> For my part, says God, I know of nothing in all the world as
>   lovely
> As some young kid chatting with the good God
> At the bottom of the garden ...
> A little person telling his troubles to the good God.
> I tell you, the consolations he gets
> Come directly and properly from me.

There is nothing in all creation as beautiful as a child falling asleep saying his prayers. The stars in the sky and the four seasons and the Gothic cathedrals are all glorious, but there is a higher splendour in the Catholic home:

> I tell you, says God, I know of nothing as beautiful in all the
>   world
> As a small child falling asleep as he says his prayers
> Under the wing of his guardian angel
> And who smiles at the angels as he begins to fall asleep,
> Who mixes everything up and doesn't understand anything
> And gets the words of the 'Our Father' wrong and goes
>   pell-mell through
> the words of the Hail Mary.[53]

Why is the sleepy prayer of the child so beautiful? Because the 'little being' goes to sleep in total confidence in our Father who is in Heaven. Péguy, in his catechetical simplicity, intuited what some theologians, in their ideological complexity, ignore: the baptized child is a divinized man, a young saint,[54] inwardly and profoundly sanctified by Habitual Grace, the Infused Virtues, and the Gifts of the Holy Spirit. Long before he can apprehend the fact by conscious and deliberate acts, the

[53] Ibid., 789f.
[54] St Pius X, the Pope who restored Holy Communion to young children, once said: 'There will be saints among the children!'

baptized infant is in living communion with the Trinity. As St Thomas Aquinas says, when explaining why the Sacrament of Confirmation can be conferred on young children:

> Bodily age does not prejudice the soul, and so even in the age of childhood men can receive the perfection of spiritual age, of which it is said: 'Venerable old age is not that of long time, nor counted by the number of years' (Wis. 4:8). That is why many in the age of childhood, through the strength of the Holy Spirit that they have received, have contended for Christ, even to the shedding of blood.[55]

Freed from Original Sin and still innocent of actual sin, the baptized child rests, as in a cradle, within the state of grace. In the poet's words, 'Heaven lies about us in our infancy'.[56] The seven Gifts of the Holy Spirit make the infant's soul beautifully responsive to divine inspirations.[57] 'If no obstacle is placed in his way, the soul of the little Christian will normally, by the *élan* of its charity, tend ever more strongly towards God.'[58] His mother and father must help him walk, without stumbling, into the age of reason. They must teach and show him how to exercise the virtues, theological and moral, so that, as Sister Jeanne d'Arc once wrote, he may as an adult rediscover 'that familiarity with the supernatural, that intuition of the things of God, that ready docility towards grace, which [he] had so spontaneously when [he was] small'.[59] Paradoxically, it is through the 'adult' virtue of prudence that he will become, or remain, a child in his faith, hope, and charity. Childish imprudence in relation to creatures will destroy childlike abandonment to God.[60] If we are 'mere children' in the world, it will seduce us with its 'cunning craftiness'. To be as simple as doves

---

[55] *Summa theologiae*, 3a 72, 8, ad 2.

[56] 'Ode on the Intimations of Immortality from Recollections of Early Childhood', *The Poetical Works of Wordsworth*, p. 588.

[57] According to St Thomas, the Gifts of the Holy Spirit dispose us 'to become readily moveable by divine inspiration' (*Summa theologiae*, 1a2ae 68, 1).

[58] Bruno de Jésus-Marie OCD, 'L'enfant et la voie de l'enfance', *Études carmélitaines* 19 (1934), 20.

[59] 'Les petits enfants et l'oraison', *L'anneau d'or* 83 (1958), 386.

[60] See the interesting article by V. de Couesnongle OP, 'Vertus d'enfance et maturité', *La vie spirituelle* 366 (1951), 273–294.

towards God, we must be as wise as serpents towards the world (cf. Matt. 10:16).

Little Girl Hope

According to Péguy, the theological virtue that children by nature symbolize and by grace embody so perfectly is the 'second virtue', Christian hope, which he defines with the Thomistic precision of his Catechism: 'Hope is a supernatural virtue by which we confidently expect from God His grace in this life and eternal glory in the next.'[61] Hope thus defined is like a child, a young lass:

> Faith is a faithful wife,
> Charity is a mother,
> An ardent mother, full of heart,
> Or an older sister who is like a mother.
> Hope is a little slip of a girl,
> Who came into the world on Christmas Day last year.[62]

Péguy's intuitions are in harmony with the thinking of St Thomas Aquinas, who in the *Prima Secundae* of the *Summa Theologiae* sets out the reasons for the natural hopefulness of the young. They have little past to look back on, he says, and plenty of future to look forward to. They are ardent and enthusiastic and so ready for any task, however arduous. They have faced few setbacks, so they feel they can do anything.[63] All that is good in this natural tendency of the young is reproduced supernaturally in men of every age through the infused theological virtue of hope. Even as his earthly life draws to a close, in the hour of his final agony, the Christian can still hope – for eternal happiness in the Vision of God, the Communion of Saints, the Resurrection of the Body, and Life Everlasting.[64]

Christian hope is the principle of spiritual rejuvenation. As Balthasar says, 'while all things in the world sink down toward the entropy of death, hope is the only thing that swims against

[61] Porche, OPC 537.
[62] Ibid., 536. Cf. Innocents, OPC 677f.
[63] Cf. *Summa theologiae*, 1a2ae 40, 6.
[64] Ibid., 2a2ae 17, 2.

the stream and moves upward'.[65] The child is audacious and undaunted, and so is the hopeful Christian. Every day is a fresh start. 'Every morning, when [children] get up, they believe the day will be good.'[66] Though he admits that without Christ he can do nothing, the childlike soul is sure he can do all things in Him who strengthens him (cf. Phil. 4:13). He storms Heaven with his prayers. Like the Hound of Heaven and unlike the mad dogs of heresy (a Calvin, a Jansen), the true Catholic does not give up on anyone: he is willing to pray for the repentance of every breathing sinner and for the purgation of any departed soul. He knows nothing of double predestination, of an unconditional positive reprobation. God has no hit-lists. Hope makes the Catholic feel something of what the Heart of the Good Shepherd feels when He searches for the lost sheep.[67] When there is charity as well as hope in his heart, a man can hope for the final bliss of his loved ones.[68] It was these truths of traditional orthodoxy that soothed the soul of Péguy. His doubts about eternal punishment were resolved in a simple and child-like way. This man of the Catechism, this proudly parochial Catholic, did not want to construct the signposts of his faith, as the Protestants do; he was content with the ones the Church herself had given him.[69] He had no truck with Origenism or any other explaining away of Hell.[70] It was

---

[65] Balthasar, op. cit., p. 859.

[66] Porche, OPC 629. See pp. 108f. below on the theme of morning in Bernanos.

[67] 'In the very heart of God, / In the heart of Jesus. / The trembling of fear and the shudder, / The shiver of hope' (Porche, OPC 571). Péguy's words could be misunderstood. According to St Thomas, Jesus, through the Beatific Vision that He enjoyed from His conception, had the full possession of God, and so He did not have hope for that possession. However, He did hope for the immortality and glory of His body (cf. *Summa theologiae*, 3a 7, 4). Péguy is describing poetically the Sacred Heart's zeal for souls. It is this which the Christian heart shares by the theological virtues of hope and charity.

[68] 'Presupposing one's union with love with another person, one can desire and hope for something for someone else as for oneself. In this way one can hope for eternal life for another person, inasmuch as one is united to him through love' (*Summa theologiae*, 2a2ae 17, 3).

[69] 'Note conjointe sur M. Descartes', OPR 2, 1553f.

[70] 'Our Catechism was written for little kids and not for us grown-ups' ('Note conjointe sur M. Descartes', OPR 2, 1542).

enough for Péguy that he could pray and hope for his friends without reserve.[71]

Péguy's doctrine of Christian hope, of hope against Hell, preserves his praise of childhood from distortion by cuteness, saves it from death by *kitsch*. Hope is a child, but she does not tread the primrose path. She follows the Lamb to the slaughter. She does not flinch even when she sees the stars falling from the heavens, but cries out with the voice of the Bride: 'Amen. Come, Lord Jesus' (Apoc. 22:20). All shall be well.

> The praise of childhood, which could have been no more than remorse, is gradually transformed into praise of 'Little Girl Hope', born anew every moment, restoring youth in the aged heart, capable of giving a new childhood to the age of misery and degeneration. What Péguy, and with him the Joan of Arc of the *Mystères* taught by Madame Gervaise, gradually came to see is that the Eternal really is present in every moment of time; and that this consoling certainty, which saves the world from Time, is based, centred, on the Christian dogma of the Incarnation and the promises it contains.[72]

The Mother of the Child

Children need mothers. That law of nature was fulfilled supernaturally when the crucified Son of God gave His Virgin Mother to St John and in him to all the members of His Mystical

---

[71] In both *Jeanne d'Arc*, written before he regained his faith, and *Le mystère de la charité de Jeanne d'Arc*, Madame Gervaise tells Joan: 'We never know if our prayer [for some soul] is in vain' (OPC 42, 524). In other words, in this life we do not know whether a prayer said for a departed soul is in vain because the soul is in Hell rather than in Purgatory. However, in the Catholic text, Péguy makes Madame Gervaise utter these words 'with great feeling, as a muffled cry, as a secret cry', as the expression of a deep and costly mystery. Then she adds this magnificent correction: 'Or rather we know that prayer is never in vain. There is the treasury of prayer. Ever since Jesus said His Our Father. Since the first time Jesus said the Our Father' (OPC 524). I do not believe that any statement can be found in Péguy's writings that is compatible with Balthasar's problematic speculations about Hell (the theory that Divine Revelation only ever presents Hell to us as a possibility rather than an actuality for human souls). I therefore find myself in disagreement with Father Dejond's interpretation (cf. pp. 112ff.).

[72] *Prière*, p. 37.

Body (cf. John 19:26f.). Just as in and through Christ we become children of His heavenly Father, so in and through Him we are children of His human Mother: '*Mater Dei*, Mother of God, / Mother of Jesus and of all men His brethren.'[73] Charles Péguy was a grateful child of Mary. Two days before his death in the great battle of the Marne, he laid his life at the Virgin's feet and strewed late summer flowers on her altar. He owed the Mediatrix nothing less than everything, the whole saving grace of her Son. 'Our Lady has saved me from despair ... In the mechanism of salvation the *Ave Maria* is our final help; with it, it is impossible not to be saved.'[74] Hope is indeed a little girl. Hope is a young maiden, Blessed Mary Ever-Virgin. *Spes nostra, salve.*

Chartres Cathedral, the destination of Péguy's famous pilgrimage, houses a priceless relic, the Veil of the Virgin. In the Church's Tradition, especially in the icons of the East, this sacred cloth, stretched out, is a sign of Our Lady's over-arching intercession for her pilgrim sons on earth. Péguy believed that his entire existence had been covered by this roof of loving kindness. It was his heaven-haven and safest home:

> *Advocata nostra*, what we seek
> Is the shelter of a shining mantle,
> *Et spes nostra, salve*, what we shall find
> Is the gate and access of a shining castle.[75]

As Charles Péguy journeyed from what he saw as an uneventful nineteenth century towards the expected cataclysms of the twentieth, he felt the protecting presence of the Woman who is Christian hope in her very person. It was to her that he commended his children when they were sick, 'for the Son took all the sins, but the Mother took all the sorrows'.[76] The Blessed Virgin is ever near. Glorified in body as well as soul, she is close to all that is material and ordinary in our daily life, 'infinitely heavenly, / Because she is also infinitely earthly ... infinitely above us, / Because she is infinitely among us ... infinitely far /

---

[73] Innocents, OPC 564.
[74] *Lettres et entretiens* (Paris, 1927), p. 174.
[75] Ève, OPC 1107.
[76] Porche, OPC 558.

Because she is infinitely close'.[77] The high Queen of Heaven is most humbly down-to-earth. That is why peasant places like the Beauce, with its golden sea of wheatfields, have a special place in her heart:

> O Star of the Sea, behold the broad expanse,
> And the deep swell and the ocean of wheat,
> And the moving foam and our loaded barns –
> Cast now thine eyes upon this immense cope.[78]

In his epic *Ève*, Péguy rhymes *charnel*, 'fleshly', with *maternel*, 'motherly'.[79] This has a dogmatic point. The Son of God is flesh of our flesh because He is flesh of the flesh of the Virgin: she is 'His Mother in the works of the Spirit and His fleshly Mother'.[80] In the middle of *Ève*, Péguy abruptly breaks the rhythm of his repetitions and states the *factum* of the *Verbum caro*: 'And Jesus is the fruit of a mother's womb.'[81] When the Father's mighty Word leapt from singing Heaven to silent earth, He placed Himself in dependency on a mother, first in the womb and later at the breast. This lowly maiden 'carried, gave birth to, suckled, carried in her arms, Him who died for the sins of the world'.[82]

Like the sculptors and glaziers of Chartres, Péguy discovers types and shadows of Our Lady on every page of the Old Law. The Mother of God is the Virgin Daughter of Zion, Israel's fairest flower. Thus, since He took flesh from a 'poor Jewess of Judea', God the Son became not simply man, but Jew, Son of David, Son of Abraham. Péguy proves that the Christian has a higher esteem for the Jews than the Jews could ever have for themselves, for the Christian must confess what no Jew would dare utter: the God of Israel is Himself a Son of Israel and was circumcised on the eighth day.

Péguy envied the Jews their bonds of blood with the God-Man: 'We are brothers of Jesus in our humanity. But you Jews were his brothers in His very family. / Brothers of His race and

---

[77] Ibid., 572.
[78] Beauce, OPC 896.
[79] See Béguin, *L'Ève de Péguy*, p. 117.
[80] Mystère, OPC 477.
[81] Ève, OPC 1043.
[82] Mystère, OPC 476.

of the same line. On you He poured out unique tears.'[83] These lines are a counterblast to all Marcionism and anti-Semitism, especially to that shameful hatred of the Jews which was poured out in Péguy's life-time in the wake of the Dreyfus case.[84] Péguy's thought is echoed in the magnificent words of his contemporary, Léon Bloy, the godfather of his friends, the Maritains, a man whom, sadly, in this life he did not come to love:

> Anti-Semitism is the most horrible blow that Our Lord has received in His everlasting Passion. It is the bloodiest and the most unpardonable, because He receives it on the face of His Mother and from the hand of Christians.[85]

Péguy and Bloy show how the Church's orthodox Christology, of which her Mariology is an essential part, is the foundation of that 'spiritual Semitism' which, according to Pope Pius XI, is inseparable from Christian faith and Baptism. They unsheathed their spiritual swords in the defence of those who have been the Devil's selected target this century, the common victims of his hellish holocaust, the two groups that to his fury remind him of the Woman and her Seed: the Jewish people (ever a child among the nations, cf. Hos. 11:1) and all the little ones of the world.

Those who love Mary as Mother become more childlike in their approach to Jesus and the Father. This truth dawns upon Péguy as he looks at the faces of his fellow-pilgrims in the cathedral:

> This is the place where everyone becomes a child,
> Especially this old man with his grey beard

---

[83] Ibid., 411f.

[84] In 'Notre Jeunesse', Péguy says that the Dreyfus affair 'was an outstanding crisis in three histories that are themselves outstanding. It was an outstanding crisis in the history of Israel. It was an outstanding crisis, of course, in the history of France. It was above all an outstanding crisis, and this dignity will become more and more apparent, it was above all an outstanding crisis in the history of Christianity' (OPR 2, 537).

[85] A letter of 2 January 1910 cited by Albert Béguin in *Léon Bloy. Mystique de la douleur* (Paris, 1948), p. 41.

> And his breeze-roughed hair
> And his modest and once triumphant eyes.[86]

The grace of spiritual infancy is not only the secret that fills Mary's heart as Temple of the Holy Spirit, but the gift that she mediates as Mother of the Church. It is the Immaculate Conception which makes her so young in spirit, 'younger than sin', as Georges Bernanos, Péguy's spiritual son and heir, will say.[87] Here is the furnace from which the fire of Péguy's thought blazes up:

> Every question, spiritual and temporal, eternal and fleshly, gravitates round a central point, about which I never cease to think, and which is the keystone of my religion. That point is the Immaculate Conception.[88]

In Mary Immaculate, the eternal and young God puts a stop to the downward rush of fallen human life, to the decline towards corruption and the degradation into sin. From the first moment of her existence, through the anticipated merits of her Son, the Blessed Virgin's soul is free from the decrepitude of Original Sin. She is 'infinitely little' and 'infinitely young', says Péguy, using words that reach back to St Louis de Montfort and are echoed in St Thérèse.[89] By succumbing to Satan's temptation, Adam was inveigled into an illusory adulthood of rebellion, thereby robbing himself and us of the free gift of original innocence, of a communion with the Trinity blessed with 'native purity, youthful purity, pristine purity, created purity, infant purity'.[90] The Lord's little Handmaid is innocent of all sin from her conception and for ever. Not only does she never lose her childhood's innocence, she is even conceived immaculate and remains for ever engraced with 'youthful purity, infant purity'. Here is the beginning of beginnings, the freshest of fresh starts. By the grace of the Holy Spirit, for the sake of the eternal Son

---

[86] Cinq prières, OPC 913.

[87] See p. 117 below.

[88] Notre Dame (Paris, 141), p. 7. Father Léthel praises the pages in the Porche on Our Lady's purity as 'among the loveliest ever written about the Immaculate Conception' (Connaître, p. 447).

[89] See pp. 51f. above.

[90] Porche, OPC 575.

whom incarnate she bears, Mary Immaculate is never anything
but the Father's innocent adopted daughter. And not only is
she from her conception ever young in soul, she is also ever
young in body from her Assumption. The rejuvenating power
of the risen Son transfigures her flesh, at the end of her earthly
life, into an eternal and unfading youth:

> And only two bodies have returned from the world
> Intact, pure, girded fresher than a baby,
> And two bodies have left the sordid round
> Brighter than wheat on harvest eve.[91]

In his *Présentation de la Beauce*, Péguy thinks of Purgatory
as the cleansing pain endured by sin-aged souls when they
glimpse, from afar, the ageless beauty of the Virgin:

> We ask for nothing more, Refuge of Sinners,
> Than the last place in your Purgatory
> Where at length we may bewail our tragic history
> And behold from afar your youthful splendour.[92]

The Mother of God in the 'youthful splendour' of her holiness is nearer to us than she would be in the antique dullness of
sin. Wickedness separates; but holiness unites. Grace makes a
man, even Methuselah, a son-in-the-Son, with a child's heart
that is open to all. Sin makes even a boy an old hack and serf of
Satan, imprisoned in self and closed to friendship. She who is
full of grace from her conception is closer to each and all of us
than any sullied son of Adam could ever be. Her privileged
intimacy with the Three Divine Persons grants her a unique
sympathy with all human persons.

> Some day we have to go back
> ... To her who is infinitely above us
> Because she is also infinitely among us ...
>
> To her who is with us,
> Because the Lord is with her.

---

[91] Suite d'Ève, OPC 1420.
[92] Beauce, OPC 907.

To her who intercedes,
Because she is blessed among all women,
And Jesus, the fruit of her womb, is blessed ...

To her who is infinitely queen
Because she was a poor woman, a destitute woman,
a poor Jewess of Judea ...
To her who is infinitely far
Because she is infinitely close.

To her who is the highest princess
Because she is the humblest woman.

To her who is closest to God
Because she is the closest to men.[93]

Péguy cannot separate Mary in his mind from Eve, Mary's mother and type. 'Only two women have been pure being carnal. And have been carnal being pure, Eve and Mary. Eve till sin, Mary eternally.'[94] Eve was the first woman to grow grey in sin, the first to be subject to decay. Péguy's heart goes out to her: 'O Mother buried outside the first garden!'[95] Modernism gloatingly denies the historicity of our first parents. The Catholic Péguy, by contrast, re-affirms their reality and their role in the drama of redemption. He not only helps our minds to understand them, but stirs our hearts to revere them, for, as he knows well, in Jewish and Catholic Tradition, Adam and Eve are not only the first sinners to lose their innocence but the first penitents to plead for forgiveness, and it was for their deliverance from Hell that their Son and God descended from Heaven. As Albert Béguin says so beautifully: 'Eve too, whom Péguy includes in the company of intercessors, is precious to him as mother of men and as the prefiguration of the Mother of God, but above all because she is the one who, having known original purity, was the first to be subjected to the law of aging.'[96] Chesterton, too, honoured, out of piety, the first Mother of the Living and connected her with her greater daughter, the Mother of the living God:

[93] Porche, OPC 572.
[94] Innocents, OPC 742.
[95] Ève, OPC 935.
[96] Béguin, Prière, pp. 48f.

But the Lord looked down on the beauty of Woman shattered,
                    A fallen sky,
Crying 'O crown and wonder and world's desire
                    Shall this too die?
Lo, it repenteth me that this too is taken;
                    I will repay,
I will repair and repeat of the ancient pattern
                    Even in this clay.[97]

Child of the Church

Charles Péguy is a child of the Church, the Catholic Church
that for him is at once Jewish and Roman.[98] He cannot fail to
love her who is the Father's chosen daughter, the Son's dear
Bride, and, in the Holy Spirit, every Christian's kind Mother.
After all, her doctrine and discipline have divine guarantees:

> I will not let my Church fall short, says God,
> I will not let her err, I will not let her fail ...
> I am involved as much in the commandments of the Church
> as in my own commandments.[99]

When Péguy thinks of the Church, it is above all the parish
that he has in mind. However poor and obscure, his local
church, like every other in Catholic Christendom, holds a
treasure outweighing silver and gold: the real, true, and sub-
stantial presence of the God-Man – Body, Blood, Soul and
Divinity – under the species of bread. Péguy praises the
Eucharistic Jesus with words worthy of the Curé d'Ars:

> He is there.
> He is there as on the first day.
> He is there among us as on the day of His death ...
> His body, the same body, hangs on the same Cross;
> His eyes, His same eyes, tremble with the same tears
> His blood, His same blood, bleeds from the same wounds;

[97] 'The Return of Eve', Mackey, pp. 160f.

[98] The 'chain' connecting all Catholic life is both Jewish and Roman. 'Thus
my Roman liturgy is linked with my central and cardinal preaching / And to
my Judean prophecy. / And the chain is Jewish and Roman' (Innocents, OPC
796).

[99] Innocents, OPC 801.

His heart, His same heart, bleeds with the same love.
The same sacrifice makes the same blood flow,
A parish has shone with an eternal brilliance. But every parish
    shines eternally, for in
every parish there is the Body of Jesus Christ.[100]

The sad irony is that, though he regained his faith, Péguy's irregular marriage barred him from receiving the Body of Jesus Christ in Holy Communion. His wife was an unbeliever, and he would not force her into a Church wedding, nor would he put pressure on her to convert.[101] Only at the end, on the eve of battle, did Péguy return to the Sacraments.[102] Despite his devotion to the Blessed Sacrament, Péguy felt no bitterness at his separation from the altar. Unlike those in our own day who campaign against the Church's law on Marriage and the Eucharist, he was even able to see a positive meaning in his situation. Though not technically an 'excommunicate', he accepted the name. Even an excommunicate, so he thought, could have an ecclesial mission: 'The excommunicate is definitely not outside the Church, because he bears on himself the mark of the Church, because he bears, as a witness, because he retains on himself the trace, the mark, of a Church penalty ... He is like a perpetual witness ... The proof is that he can come back. He can go back into the City.'[103] Somewhat like St. Andrew the Holy Fool in the Russian icon of Our Lady's Veil, Péguy is a wild man on the Church's edge, pointing to the still centre of the City that is both Rome and Jerusalem. This marginal layman, who witnessed to Catholic truth in a hostile

[100] Mystère, OPC 412. In 1986 Pope John Paul II devoted his annual Holy Thursday 'Letter to Priests' to St John Vianney in commemoration of the second centenary of his birth. The Holy Father said this of the Curé's devotion to the Blessed Sacrament: 'It was generally before the tabernacle that he spent long hours in adoration, before daybreak or in the evening; it was towards the tabernacle that he often turned during his homilies, saying with emotion: "He is there!"' (Letters to My Brother Priests 1979–1991 [Chicago, 1992], p. 166).

[101] After his death, she became a Catholic, and their children were baptized.

[102] On the Feast of the Assumption 1914 he heard Mass in the little parish church of Loupmont. He almost certainly made his confession and received Holy Communion on the same occasion (see the note of P. Péguy, OPC xli).

[103] Véronique, OPR 2, 426.

secular sphere, is more truly an *anima ecclesiastica* than the clericalized laymen and laicized clerics who do nothing but criticize the Pope.

There was nothing easy about Péguy's Catholic fidelity. There was more than a little anti-clericalism in his passionate soul. In the Church, as in marriage, he had to struggle to be faithful, as we can see in Joan's effort to heed the counsel of Madame Gervaise (the figure of the teaching Church) in 'The Mystery of the Charity of Joan of Arc':

> What the *Mystère de la charité* shows us is an initially restive Péguy, or at least an obstinately uneasy one, close to despair, who finally finds peace (which does not mean going to sleep) by giving his assent to the Church, by letting himself be taught by her and uniting himself to the prayer of all. Jeannette is 'taught by Madame Gervaise', who makes her see 'little by little' what 'the Christian dogma of the Incarnation' involves.[104]

Although he loved the visible Church Militant on earth, both in her parochial littleness and in her universal Roman grandeur, he cherishes no less the Church Suffering in Purgatory and the Church Triumphant in Heaven. Of the Poor Souls, Madame Gervaise says:

> For them, to their profit, we can, we must, multiply our work, our prayers, our sufferings. Our merits, if we can steal that word from Jesus Christ, His unique merits. The merits of Jesus Christ. Our fathers and the fathers of our father may be there. God has their soul. To work for them, to pray for them, suffer for them. Merit for them. That is the law, that is the rule.[105]

To pray for the souls in Purgatory, to offer up for them the afflictions of daily life, is the connatural act of a childlike Catholic heart, 'the natural movement of our love, of our human love, of our familial love, of our filial love'.[106] The Holy Souls are our fathers and mothers, our brothers and sisters, our kinsmen in Christ. To deny them our suffrages would be dire and unnatural cruelty.

[104] H. de Lubac and J. Bastaire, *Claudel et Péguy* (Paris, 1974), p. 92.
[105] Mystère, OPC 429.
[106] Ibid.

To the Church Triumphant, Péguy's heart soars up on wings of hope: 'We must strive to belong to her ... We must pray to [the saints] for others and for ourselves – we can do it openly – pray to them, for those who belong to the Church Suffering and those who belong to the Church Militant.'[107] The Christian's first school, his natural environment for learning and loving, is the Communion of Saints. 'He sees himself under the gaze, under the consideration, and not so much under the judgement as under the protection of innumerable earlier saints, innumerable patrons.'[108] Jesus is the Head of the Communion of Saints (His Mystical Body's loveliest name). All His and His saints' virtues, all their prayers and trials and merits, are laid up as a treasury for all Christendom, for the salvation of all the world.[109]

During the last thirty years, the Church has been plagued with schemes of religious education that flaunt their modernity and pour scorn on the methods of the past, especially the question-and-answer catechism. Modernist educators take pleasure in repudiating the manner in which they themselves were once formed in the faith. They speak as though there were an unbridgeable gulf, in their own as well as the Church's life, between the pre- and post-conciliar periods. *Aggiornamento* has come to mean the loss of Catholic memory, estrangement from our fathers in the faith. By contrast, Péguy saw the prayers and catechism of his childhood as the permanent inspiration of his adult thinking and living: 'All I did not know on the morning of my First Communion, I shall never know.'[110] Like everything childlike and simple, these sources are of inexhaustible richness and unfathomable depth. If the Church is to fashion a new catechetics, she would do well to listen to her son, Charles Péguy.

Father and Soldier

There is nothing unmanly about Péguy's praise of childhood. It is not the sickly-sweet sentimentality which oozed through

[107] 'Clio', OPR 2, 219.
[108] Mystère, OPC 429.
[109] Ibid., 390.
[110] 'Note conjointe sur M. Descartes', OPR 2, 1542. Cf. Laudet, OPR 2, 903.

Victorian and Edwardian literature and was often the work of disordered minds. Péguy's theology of childhood is, first of all, a father's wise understanding and kindly love of children. To be a *paterfamilias*, said Péguy, is the most adventurous calling in the cosmos, because the whole culture of modernity is organized in opposition to the man who has the audacity to marry a wife and beget children.[111] Péguy was convinced that no sane man would have the heart to go out to work except for his children. All he wants is his children's happiness: 'You live for them, all you ask is that your children be happy.' He trembled when he thought of the time they were ill and he placed them in the arms of Our Lady.[112] Secondly, this doctrine of spiritual infancy is the achievement, not of an armchair aesthete, a 'pale intellectual',[113] but of a courageous soldier, who died in the first great battle of the First World War – a providential honour for the man who loved beginnings. This father and soldier was in a great tradition of Christian chivalry, of Galahad and Roland, of St Louis and St Joan:

> Blessed are they who died for the fleshly earth,
> Provided it was in a just war.
> Blessed are they who died for a plot of ground.
> Blessed are they who died a solemn death.
>
> Blessed are they who died in great battles,
> Abed upon the sod in the face of God ...
>
> Blessed are they who died in a just war.
> Blessed the ripe ears and the wheat in sheaves for harvest.[114]

Péguy displayed what Chesterton regarded as the unmistakable mark of the French Catholic: *militancy*: 'There is nothing apologetic about [the French Catholic's] apologetics ... To put this aspect of French Catholicism in a word, in France the defence is not merely defensive. It is, in the honourable and

---

[111] 'Everything is against the head of a family, against the father of a family, and consequently against the family itself, against the life of the family' (Véronique, OPR 2, 374).

[112] Cf. Porche, OPC 556.

[113] 'Note conjointe sur M. Descartes', OPR 2, 1522.

[114] Ève, OPC 1028.

soldierly sense of the word, offensive. As Mr. Belloc has re-
marked somewhere, the French do not fight with reluctance.'[115]
Nor did Péguy. All his poetry and prose, not least his writings about childhood, are the thunderous cannonade of a man
who believed that every Christian is a soldier of Christ. There
is a spiritual war going on, he cries out, and none of the
baptized must leave his post. 'For our wrestling is not against
flesh and blood, but against principalities and powers, against
the rulers of the world of this darkness, against the spirits of
wickedness in the high places' (Eph. 6:12). Péguy flung his
steel gauntlet into Modernism's satin salon of appeasement:
'*Miles Christi*, Today every Christian is a soldier, the soldier of
Christ. There are no more tranquil Christians ...The holy war is
everywhere. It is ever being waged. Today we are all posted to
the front line. We are all on the front line. The front line is
everywhere.'[116]

The good God gave Péguy the prophetic grace to see that
Satan's warfare is waged in a special way against children, for
they personify the dispositions of humility and obedience
needed for entry to God's Kingdom, the virtues which the
demons most despise and do their utmost to destroy: 'Amen I
say to you, whosoever shall not receive the Kingdom of God as
a little child shall not enter into it' (Mark 10:15). Herod, the
slaughterer of the babes of Bethlehem, is the Devil's archetypal
accomplice, and his victims, the Holy Innocents, enjoy a
primatial glory among the martyrs.

> And the Apostle calls them *primitiae Deo, et Agno*, first fruits to
> God and to the Lamb. That is to say, first fruits of the earth
> offered to God and to the Lamb. The other saints are ordinary
> fruits, the fruits of the season.
> But they are the fruits
> Of the season's very promise.
>
> And following the Apostle, the Church repeats: *Innocentes pro
> Christo
> infantes occisi sunt,*

[115] 'The Challenge of the Curé d'Ars' in Henry Ghéon, *The Secret of the Curé
d'Ars* (New York, 1929), pp. 212f.
[116] Laudet, OPR 2, 966ff.

> Innocents for Christ
> the children were massacred
> (*infantes*, very young children, a tiny child not yet speaking).[117]

God the Father sees all children in His Son, His Son in all children, but the Innocents of Bethlehem resemble the Only-Begotten in a unique way, for they are His contemporaries and compatriots, as well as His comrades in the infant state of His human nature:

> I love them innocently, says God ...
> (That's the way you should love these innocents)
> As a father of a family loves the playmates of his son
> Who go to school with him.[118]

The Holy Innocents of Bethlehem are united with the Son, and confess His Incarnation, simply by the fact of their infancy and the time and place of their birth, and through this bond they are sanctified by the Holy Spirit, dying a death that is true martyrdom, a Baptism in Blood that confers the salvific effects of Baptism in Water. This is the doctrine of Pope St Leo the Great, preaching on the Solemnity of the Epiphany:

> They were able to die for Him whom they could not yet confess. Thus Christ, so that no period of His life should be without miracle, silently exercised the power of the Word before the use of speech, as if already saying, 'Suffer the little children and forbid them not to come to me, and do not hinder them, for the Kingdom of Heaven is for such' (Matt. 19:14). He crowned infants with a new glory, and consecrated the first days of these little ones by His own beginnings, in order to teach us that no member of the human race is incapable of the divine mystery, since even this age was capable of the glory of martyrdom.[119]

Quoting Prudentius's hymn sung by the Church on their feast day, Péguy shows how the Holy Innocents reveal the true character of Paradise. It is a playground. The Holy Innocents

---

[117] Innocents, OPC 820.
[118] Ibid., 819.
[119] *In Epiphaniae solemnitate sermo 2*, n. 3; SC 22B. 224.

romp in the nurseries of Heaven, in the nursery of God's sons, which is what Heaven is:

Vox prima Christi victima,
Grex immolatorum tener,
Aram sub ipsam simplices
Palma et coronis luditis.
First victim of Christ,
Tender flock of the immolated
Simple at the altar's foot,
Simplices, simple souls, simple children,
Palma et coronis luditis. You play with the palm and the crowns,
With your palm and your crowns.

Such is my paradise, says God. My paradise is all that is
   simplest.
Nothing is as unpretentious as my paradise
Aram sub ipsam, at the foot of the very altar
These simple children *play* with their palm and their martyrs'
   crowns
That's what goes on in my Paradise.[120]

For Prudentius and Péguy, as also for Dante, the merriment of 'unpretentious' Paradise, the blissful act of beholding the Trinity, is a kind of play.[121] Spiritual childhood is not only the way to Heaven, it is Heaven's very life.

The battle which Péguy fought for innocence and the Innocents still rages. It is the central struggle of our century, compared with which the clash of nations and ideologies are trifling skirmishes. Péguy's call to arms, issued in the spirit of Christian chivalry, defines both the end and the means of the fight. The end is the glory of the Triune God and the defence of the least of Christ's brethren, and the means are the virtues of the Little Way, a childlike exercise of Faith, Hope, and Charity (accompanied, as we have seen, by a manly exercise of the moral virtues). To defend the Innocents we must strive, by God's grace, to be like them. By artless fidelity to the truth in a world of adult deceit, by a humble confidence that disarms the giants of despair, by a prodigal love of the smallest of our brethren,

---

[120] Innocents, OPC 823.
[121] '. . . l'ultimo è tutto d'Angelici ludi' (*Paradiso*, Canto 28, 126).

we follow the Lamb wherever He goes. Our simplicity will be our strength.[122] This is the true 'mystery of the charity of Joan of Arc', France's boldest warrior and youngest saint, and it is the final paradox of Péguy's Christian theology of childhood: only the Lamb-like learn the secret of the Lion.

> These follow the Lamb wherever He goes.
>
> *Hi sequuntur Agnum quocumque ierit,*
> *Hi empti sunt.* Again. They were purchased. Were carried off.
>
> *Hi empti sunt ex hominibus,*
>
> These were carried off from men,
> (From among men, from the presence of men),
>
> *primitiae Deo, et Agno,*
>
> first-fruits to God, and to the Lamb:
>
> *et in ore eorum non est inventum mendacium,*
>
> and in their mouth,
> and on their lips no lie was found;
>
> (The lie of man, the adult lie, the earthly lie.
> The soiled lie.
> The dirty lie).
> *sine macula enim sunt ante thronum Dei,*
>
> They are without spot before the throne of God.[123]

Appendix

Péguy was not an impostor. He recognized himself to be a sinner. I have tried not to beatify him in this chapter. I admire him, but I do not presume to think that he is already in Heaven, and so I pray for his brave soul, as he would wish, that God grant him eternal rest and shine perpetual light upon him. Yet, while not a saint, Péguy was, in my opinion, a prophet in the

---

[122] Preaching on the feast of St Stephen, St Bonaventure says: 'Grace is an influence calling the soul back to its first simplicity. Now the simpler something is, the stronger (*virtuosius*) it is, and the stronger it is, the braver it is. Therefore, since Stephen was full of grace, he was full of fortitude' (*De Sancto Stephano martyr sermo* 1, 2; *Sancti Bonaventurae opera omnia*, vol. 9 [Quaracchi, 1901], p. 480).

[123] Innocents, OPC 806f.

strict sense, a man given by God the charism of prophecy. There is no contradiction in the two statements I have just made: for the receiving of a *gratia gratis data*, neither heroic virtue nor the state of grace is required. God can use even Balaam's ass for His messages to men.

Charles Péguy, like St Thérèse of Lisieux and G. K. Chesterton, was given a prophetic insight into the drama of the twentieth century, the 'century of wolves'. In particular, Péguy, like his two companions, was taught by God that the Holy Innocents of Bethlehem had a special significance for the coming darkness. I believe that a good argument can be made, from the writings of Péguy and Thérèse and Chesterton, that, like the Holy Innocents of Bethlehem, the myriad children slaughtered each year by abortion die as victims of an anti-Christian, anti-Christ culture of death, killed by the spiritual successors of Herod. Drawing on the teaching of Pope St Leo the Great quoted above,[124] one might then conclude that, by analogy with the Innocents of the first Year of the Lord, the Innocents of the twentieth century *anno Domini* have also died as martyrs in the strict sense. Through the very fact of their infancy, which Herod and the powers of Hell so hate, they have confessed the divine Word incarnate, and so, by a Baptism of Blood, Christ's grace of justification has been communicated to them: the guilt of Original Sin has been remitted, their souls have been sanctified inwardly, and the gates of Heaven opened up to them.

This is only a speculation. However, there seems to be some support for at least some elements of the argument in Pope John Paul II's encyclical *Evangelium vitae*. There the Holy Father says that the Child whom the Dragon seeks to devour in the vision of St John (cf. Apoc. 12:4) is 'a figure of Christ' and at the same time 'a figure of every person, every child, especially every helpless baby whose life is threatened, because, as the Council reminds us, "by His Incarnation the Son of God has united Himself in some fashion with every man"'. It is precisely in the "flesh" of every man that Christ continues to reveal Himself and to enter into fellowship with us, *so that rejection of human*

---

[124] See p. 94 above.

life, in whatever form that rejection takes, is really a rejection of Christ.
This is the fascinating but also demanding truth which Christ
reveals to us, and which His Church continues untiringly to
proclaim: "Whoever receives one such child in my name
receives me" (Matt. 18: 5); "Truly, I say to you, as you did it to
one of the least of these my brethren, you did it to me" (Matt.
25:40).'[125]

---

[125] *Evangelium vitae*, n. 104. The passage in italics is partly italicized in the
original text.

3

'Faithful to the Child I Used to Be': Bernanos and the Spirit of Childhood

Georges Bernanos had one ambition: to be true, when death came, to the little boy he once had been:

> What does my life matter? I just want it to be faithful, to the end, to the child I used to be. Yes, what honour I have, and my bit of courage, I inherit from the little creature, so mysterious to me now, scuttling through the September rain across streaming meadows, his heart heavy at the thought of going back to school.[1]

These words are not a lamentation born of nostalgia but a proclamation fired by hope. Bernanos believed that the sin of the world is the sin against childhood, and that the salvation of the world is through the spirit of childhood, by conversion in the Holy Spirit to the Child of the Virgin Mary. It is a doctrine of extraordinary richness and yet of essential simplicity. Bernanos was first and last a Christian, a Catholic, whose life as husband, father, and writer was kneaded and moulded by 'the faith of the Church, that is to say, of the whole Communion of Saints, which, through those sources of grace that are the Sacraments,

---

[1] George Bernanos, *Les grands cimetières sons la lune* (Paris, 1938), p. 79. On the theme of childhood in Bernanos, see Y. Bridel, *L'Espirit d'enfance dans l'oeuvre romanesque de Georges Bernanos* (Paris, 1966). On the suffering of the innocent, of children and the childlike, see William Bush, *Souffrance et expiation dans la pensée de Georges Bernanos* (Paris, 1962), pp. 103–125.

nourishes the living faith of believers'.[2] Both in his novels and in his many *écrits de combat*, he does no more than apply afresh the words of the Word: 'Unless you be converted and become as children, you shall not enter into the Kingdom of Heaven. Whosoever therefore shall humble himself as this Little Child, he is the greater in the Kingdom of Heaven' (Matt. 18:3f.). Fifty years after his death, as the clouds of demonic pride and child-destruction blacken the landscape of the earth, Bernanos's life and art blaze out as a beacon of Christian hope. This chapter is a torch lit from his fire.

The Demons of Old Age

According to Bernanos, the generation born after 1870 – the generation of St Thérèse, Chesterton, and Péguy – was under attack from 'the demons of old age (*vieillesse*)'.[3] This language must not be misunderstood. Bernanos is upbraiding those who are old not in years but in spirit. Like the Fathers and the Doctors of the Middle Ages, he uses the metaphor of 'young-ness' for the effects of grace and of 'oldness' for the effects of sin. A compatriot of his, the twelfth-century Cistercian, Blessed Guerric of Igny, said it all before him one Christmas Eve: 'The world had grown old; aging had brought it close to death. Suddenly, at the coming of its Creator, it found itself renewed in a new unhoped for youth and vigour, in a youthful ardour of faith.'[4]

Bernanos accepted, indeed propagated, the historical argu-ment I have presented in the previous chapters: the drama of atheistic humanism is a conspiracy against the child, always against his spirit, more and more often against his life. Now the great novelist realized that, if the strategy of modernity's war against childhood is plain, its tactics are devious. The Herods of history are too intelligent to display contempt for the child; more commonly, they exude a sycophantic interest: 'When you have found Him, bring me word again, that I also may come

---

[2] Hans Urs von Balthasar, *Le chrétien Bernanos* (Paris, 1956), p. 11.
[3] *Grands cimetières*, p. 283.
[4] *Sermo 2 in nativitate Domini*, n. 3; SC 166. 214.

and adore Him' (Matt. 2:8). In the *Journal d'un curé de campagne*, the Curé of Torcy says to the Curé of Ambricourt:

> You hear the hypocrites, the sensualists, the Scrooges, the rotten rich – with their thick lips and gleaming eyes – cooing over *Sinite parvulos*, 'Let the little children come to me', without any indication that they're taking note of the words that follow – some of the most terrible ever heard by human ears, 'If you are not like one of these little ones, you will not enter the Kingdom of God.'

In a culture of death the child is always a *thing*. When he is 'unwanted', he is discarded or destroyed. When he is 'wanted', whenever he can be employed as a means to some adult's end, then he may be flattered and pampered. Children are only ever abused when they are regarded as objects to be used. Such depersonalization is the unavoidable outcome when men cease to believe that the child is the gift of God, created in His image. The pederasty of Monsieur Ouine is, therefore, a practical atheism and the emblematic vice of the age of Antichrist.

In the style of Ouine, the totalitarian ideologies of our century have all rallied and exploited the young. Solzhenitsyn says that the most abominable face of the Gulag Archipelago in the Soviet Union was 'the maw that swallowed up the kids'. The same Stalin who consigned countless children to imprisonment and death posed in propaganda as the child's 'Best Friend'.[5] Hitler complained that older Germans were 'rotten to the core', with 'no unrestrained instincts left, bearing the burden of a humiliating past'. His hope rested entirely on those he called 'my magnificent youngsters'. Bernanos denounced this pagan adulation of youth, which was to inspire the Nazi euthanasia campaign, as a loathsome betrayal of childhood.

> They have all betrayed childhood, and yet they exploit it; they exploit its sacred symbolism. They call themselves young, they speak in the name of youth. Who now would dare to look German childhood in the face, that cruel dwarf? What has Mussolini done

[5] Alexander Solzhenitsyn, *The Gulag Archipelago*, vol. 2, 1918–1956 (ET London, 1976), pp. 431ff.

to Italian youth? As for Spanish youth, for six years it has been lapping up fresh blood from a saucer ... Yes, they have all betrayed childhood.[6]

Bernanos was suspicious even of the outwardly benign celebrations of childhood to be found in the literature of the late nineteenth century, the nostalgia for a land of lost content beyond the desert of adult disappointment. In *Un mauvais rêve*, when Emmanuel Ganse is thinking of writing up the memories of his early years, Simone Alfieri warns him against it. Literary childhood, she says, can be a flight from spiritual childhood, producing only 'fake reproductions, horrible wax dolls'. If you have anything left of your childhood, it is too precious to be squandered in print. 'It's unlikely there's enough of it left to help you live, but it will certainly aid you when you die.'[7] Bernanos does not condemn the literature of nostalgia; he is simply warning against those who, like Proust, make the psychology of brooding memory an end in itself. The recalling of childhood, for him as for Chesterton, was a means not an end, an occasion of conversion, a confession of lost innocence and a hope for a new childhood in Christ. The unbeliever snatches at the idea of childhood as a refuge from the reality of the grave, but, for the Christian Bernanos, the 'child I used to be' is not a talisman against death, but a companion on the journey through death, through the pain of Purgatory, to the happiness of Paradise.

For Bernanos, the attack on the spirit of the child is the central drama of our times, indeed of all times. In 1938, when Hitler's troops goose-stepped into Austria, he wrote: 'With the rumbling of the cannons and tanks, all the childhood of Europe has just died in Salzburg, with the young Mozart.'[8] And yet the youngness of holiness is unconquerable by the oldness of sin. Even in the last quarter of the nineteenth century, in the very years when the 'demons of old age' were plotting new offensives against the child, a Little Flower bloomed in Lisieux.

---

[6] *Lettre aux anglais* (Paris, 1948), p. 48. With his customary ambiguity, Monsieur Ouine boasts: 'I have always honoured childhood' (OR 1492).

[7] *Un mauvais rêve*, OR 919.

[8] *Grands cimetières*, p. 346.

She was sent as a doctor to heal the wounds of this century of wolves.

> It may, after all, have been among the intentions of this mysterious girl to allow our wretched world a moment of supreme respite, to give it a breathing space in the shade of its familiar mediocrity, since those little hands, innocent and terrible little hands, expert in cutting out paper flowers, though chapped to the bone by laundry chlorine, have sown a seed whose growth nothing can now stop.[9]

The Church offers not solutions but saints. These most childlike of her sons and daughters provide, as Balthasar has said, 'not a recipe but a model and an orientation, a lesson and an encouragement'.[10] Holy Mother Church, through the fatherhood of her priests, repeats the Master's call to holiness and gives her members His grace for the answering of the call, a grace at once sanctifying and rejuvenating, making saints of God, making children of God. As the Curé of Torcy reminds his young friend: 'The good God has given the Church the job of keeping the spirit of childhood alive in the world, this ingenuousness, this freshness.'[11]

The Sin Against Childhood

The sin against the spirit of childhood is, first of all, the sin against *truth*. The very name of Bernanos's most demonic character, Monsieur Ouine, symbolizes duplicity and deviousness: he is *Oui* and *Non* in one breath, a womanish man, whose every word and action seem to have a double meaning. He is the personification of ambiguity, a fitting slave of the father of lies. In contrast to the child's straightforward realism, his senescent soul pretends and makes-believe. Unlike the true child, who never confuses fact with fiction, he lives in a fantasy world. The Abbé Cénabre in *L'Imposture* is just such a pretender. He is a priest without faith, an historian of mysticism who no longer prays, a spiritual impostor. By a twist of Pascal's famous

[9] Ibid., p. 242.
[10] *Le chrétien Bernanos*, p. 26.
[11] *Journal*, OR 1046.

wager, he confesses that he needs the 'hypothesis' of God to support the life he finds most congenial. 'God is necessary for my habits, my work, my station in life. I shall act, therefore, as if He existed.'[12] Cénabre's present existence is a sham, because he is determined to slam the door on the humiliations of his childhood – the shame of being the son of an alcoholic father and the grandson of a man who died in jail.[13] The 'child he used to be' is a ghost that he wants to exorcise from the mansion of his adult mind. He hates the 'Little Way'. Even in the midst of anguish, he can find time to finish an article 'subtly and pertinently' refuting a book about St Thérèse of Lisieux.[14]

As a sin against the truth, the sin against childhood is the vice of *curiosity*. Monsieur Ouine is in despair, because the life-giving wonder of the child is dead in him; he is left with nothing but adult inquisitiveness. He is eaten up with curiosity: 'At this very moment, it gnaws and hollows out what little remains of me, Heaven knows how curious I was, but I was only hungry for souls.'[15] In *Sous le Soleil de Satan*, it is said of Antoine de Saint-Marin (alias Anatole France) that 'age has not yet blunted the sharpness of his curiosity'. *Studiositas*, the virtue that St Thomas Aquinas opposed to *curiositas*, is a devotion to the truth. It presupposes a reverent humility before the richness and splendour of being. The curious man, by contrast, refuses to serve the truth. He wants knowledge to serve him. His very mind is concupiscent, scarred by a disordered desire to know.[16] As Balthasar says:

> [Curiosity is] a knowledge without love, neither paid for nor guaranteed by any cost or trouble to oneself, the impatience of someone eager to possess right now, as if it were forbidden fruit, a vision which only divine grace can grant.[17]

[12] *L'imposture*, OR 457.

[13] Ibid., OR 364.

[14] Ibid., OR 358.

[15] *Monsieur Ouine*, OR 1557f. For a finely perceptive study of the novel, see William Bush, *L'angoisse du mystère. Essai sur Bernanos et Monsieur Ouine* (Paris, 1966).

[16] For St Thomas's discussion of *studiositas* and *curiositas*, see *Summa theologiae*, 2a2ae qq. 166 & 167.

[17] *Le chrétien Bernanos*, p. 108.

The sin-aged soul, eaten up with curiosity, is calculating and avaricious. It will not let go of itself and be caught up into love. It glorifies power and conquest, despises weakness and receptivity. And yet it remains the soul of a 'humiliated child'. The tragedy of Adolf Hitler, said Bernanos, was that he fulfilled only the ugly dreams of a self-seeking 'maturity' and not the great and beautiful dreams of childhood.[18] Even Monsieur Ouine had a childhood, till it was torn from him by a pederastic schoolmaster.[19] The Irish poet AE captures Bernanos's thought exactly:

> In ancient shadows and twilights
> Where childhood had strayed,
> The world's great sorrows were born
> And its heroes were made.
> In the lost boyhood of Judas
> Christ was betrayed.[20]

Bernanos refused to accept the authoritarian assumption, so widely held outside Christianity, that the adult is the sole measure of the human. As he grows up, a child does not become a man, a human being; he is that already, from the womb. When a woman brings forth her child, says Our Lord, 'she remembereth no more the anguish, for joy that a man is born into the world' (John 16:21). Being human is the whole journey from conception to the last breath. Moreover, in all that really matters, in faith and hope and love, the child is the teacher of the adult, the father of the man. At the end, 'a little child shall lead them' (Isa. 11:6). 'Out of the mouths of infants and of sucklings thou hast perfected praise' (Ps. 8:2). Bernanos let himself be led and perfected in praise by his own little children, as he confessed to a priest friend:

> I am waiting for a photograph of my little girl to send to you. She is a very useful director of conscience for her papa. Can one do better than imitate her? All I desire, everything scattered in the

[18] *Le chemin de la croix-des-âmes* (Paris, 1948), pp. 26–28 and passim.
[19] *Monsieur Ouine*, OR 1473.
[20] AE (George William Russell), 'Germinal', in *The Oxford Book of Modern Verse 1892–1935*. Chosen by W. B. Yeats (Oxford, 1936), p. 104. Reproduced by permission.

past, she has gathered together in her hands, and it is there that
the good Lord will find me when He deigns to call me.[21]

The Infant Word

Bernanos was led by his own little ones, was guided always by
the boy he used to be, but first of all he was led by the Lamb, the
Son given us by the Father, the Little Child that is God. Like
Péguy, Bernanos's vision of man, as both adult and child, is
Christ-centered. It is in the mystery of the God-Man that the
mystery of Everyman becomes clear to him. As he makes the
Country Priest say in his *Journal*:

> To hear us talk, you'd think that we preach the God of the
> Spiritualists, some kind of 'Supreme Being', instead of the Lord
> we have learnt to know as a marvellous and living friend, who
> suffers our pains, takes joy in our happiness, will share our agony
> and receive us into His arms, upon His heart.[22]

Bernanos revered childhood, his own and every man's,
because the Father's eternal Word, our 'marvellous and living
friend', for us became a child, conceived by the Holy Spirit and
born of the Virgin Mary. In a message for 25 December 1943,
Bernanos described Christmas Day as 'the feast of human
childhood and of the world's childhood, of all childhood united
and glorified in the heart of the Child-God'.[23] By His very life as
a child, the divine Word anticipated His later teaching as an
adult: 'Unless you be converted and become as little children,
you shall not enter into the Kingdom of Heaven' (Matt. 18:3).[24]
He comes to us in the humility with which He wants us,
through Him, to go to the Father. The Christmas mystery is,
therefore, the fitting background to several of the great testings

---

[21] Letter to Dom Besse, *Bulletin trimestriel,* 11, p. 6.

[22] *Journal,* OR 1050f.

[23] *Le chemin de la croix-des-âmes,* p. 390.

[24] As St Bernard of Clairvaux said in a Christmas Eve sermon: 'Today a
little Child is born for us, so that man may no more presume to magnify
himself, and we instead may be converted and become as little children' (*In
vigilia nativitatis Domini sermo* 5, 3; J. Leclercq OSB and H. Rochais, eds., *Sancti
Bernardi opera,* vol. 4 [Rome, 1966], p. 231).

of spiritual childhood in the works of Bernanos. For example, in *Sous le Soleil de Satan*, the 'temptation of despair', the supreme trial of the Abbé Donissan, begins on Christmas night.[25] In the *Dialogues des Carmélites*, on Christmas night, the Prioress maintains the Teresian custom of carrying the Bambino from cell to cell for the sisters to venerate. Sister Blanche, whose fear of death is at the heart of the drama, murmurs: 'How small He is, how weak!'; 'No,' says Mother Mary, 'How small He is, and how strong!' Suddenly the revolutionaries can be heard singing outside. Blanche, terrified, drops and breaks the 'Little King'. 'The Little King is dead,' she cries out, 'All we have left now is the Lamb of God.'[26] Or rather the Little King is now visible as what He has always been – the Lamb ready for the slaughter. Bernanos, like every Catholic, knows that the Sundays that follow the Infant's Epiphany are succeeded by the Sundays that lead to His Passion. From the grotto of the Nativity to the garden of the Agony, there is one sustained movement of self-humbling by the Son. In the Crib He is so little, and on the Cross He is the last and least of all. Childhood has a new dignity since the Word united it to His divine person and took it to His human heart, and human suffering, even the fear of death, has a new vocation through its assumption by that same Person and its embracing by that same Heart. As the Prioress says to her community in the *Dialogues*:

> When we look at things from the Garden of Gethsemane, where all human anguish was divinized in the precious Heart of Our Lord, the distinction between fear and courage seems to me to be almost superfluous, and both of them look like the trinkets of luxury.[27]

The World's Only Hope

The manifesto which Bernanos delivered to France in the 1930s and 1940s, and through her to the whole world, was one of spiritual childhood. Mankind's only possible path is the 'little way':

[25] OR 116ff.
[26] *Dialogues des carmélites*, OR 1656.
[27] Ibid., 1653.

The world is going to be judged by children. The spirit of childhood is going to judge the world ... Become children again, rediscover the spirit of childhood ... It's your last chance, and ours. Are you capable of rejuvenating the world, yes or no? The Gospel is always young; it is you who are old ... I have always thought that the modern world has been sinning against the spirit of youth, and that this crime would kill it.[28]

The spirit of childhood is for Bernanos what it was for St Thérèse: the disposition of a heart that expects everything from the good God as a little child expects everything from his father – in simple trust.[29] Like Péguy, Bernanos regards hope as the most childlike of the theological virtues, but he goes beyond Péguy by more sharply distinguishing natural *espoir* from supernatural *espérance*.[30] Bernanos shares Péguy's delight in the natural buoyancy of the child, but he sees that Christian hope is deeper and more costly. It is not a blithe ignorance of the agonies of existence. *Espérance* fulfils *espoir* by going into the night and only thence reaching morning:

To find hope, you must have gone beyond despair. When you get to the end of the night, you find another dawn ... Optimism is a false hope, for the use of cowards and imbeciles. Hope is a virtue, *virtus*, an heroic determination of the soul. The highest form of hope is despair surmounted.[31]

Bernanos connects childhood with the morning. When day breaks, hope is re-born. Dawn is the childlike Curé's favourite time of day: 'The deliverance of dawn is always sweet to me. It is like a grace from God, a smile. Thank God for morning!'[32]

---

[28] *Grands cimetières*, pp. 247, 262, 269, 289.

[29] See pp. 24ff. above.

[30] See pp. 79ff. above. Bernanos said that he did not deserve the comparison with Péguy, but that he would accept it because there was indeed an affinity between them like the bond between a 'humble monk' and 'the Holy Founder of his order'. In any case, it was not hard for any Frenchman to be like Péguy, 'because no one has been more French than Péguy' (*La vocation spirituelle de la France*, J.-L. Bernanos, ed. [Paris, 1975], pp. 64f.).

[31] *La liberté, pour quoi faire?* (Paris, 1953), pp. 14f. The Curé of Ambricourt shares the view of St Thomas Aquinas that the sin against hope is 'the deadliest sin of all ... the richest elixir of the devil, his ambrosia' (*Journal*, OR 1116f.). See pp. 32ff. above.

[32] *Journal*, OR 1208.

The morning is the infancy of the day, Our Lord's favoured time of prayer to the Father and the moment of His Resurrection from the tomb:

> The morning is so clear, so sweet, and of a wonderful lightness ... When I was very young, I used sometimes to snuggle down, at dawn, in one of those streaming hedges, and I went home drenched, shivering, happy, and got a slap from my poor mother, and a great bowl of boiled milk. All day, my head was filled with nothing but images of childhood.[33]

The devilish Ouine, by contrast, hates the morning. He feels the resurgence of light as an affront to the dark complacency of his self-destructiveness:

> Morning anguish is a curious kind of prolongation of insomnia. If you like, it's insomnia's insufferable full bloom. This acid freshness, this limpidity, this murmur of invisible springs, this renewal of everything, isolates more painfully than silence, than the darkness where his nerves find a calm and, so to speak, funereal security. For the morning seems to exclude him scornfully from life, to cast him out with the dead. He hates it.[34]

The Child as Poverty

The spirit of childhood is closely tied to poverty of spirit. In fact, according to the Curé of Ambricourt, they are 'without doubt one and the same thing'.[35] The reasoning is Christological rather than sociological. Poverty, like childhood, is sacred because the Son of God has made it His own: they were consecrated together in a womb in Nazareth and a manger in Bethlehem.[36] 'For you know the grace of Our Lord Jesus Christ, that being rich He became poor for your sakes, that through His poverty you might be rich' (2 Cor. 8:9). In his *Lettre aux Anglais*, Bernanos wrote:

---

[33] Ibid., p. 1114.

[34] *Monsieur Ouine*, OR 1470.

[35] *Journal*, OR 1246.

[36] 'It is by reference to Christ that the state of poverty is honourable and respectable' (Balthasar, *Le chrétien Bernanos*, p. 552).

[The hope which Christianity gives the poor] is certainly not that of a proletarian dictatorship, but of a society where the poor would be honoured, because God made Himself poor, and thus has beatified not just, as some simoniac theologians claim, the moral disposition of poverty in spirit, but the social condition of the poor.[37]

God incarnate by His poverty made blessed, as He also declared blessed, *both* the materially poor *and* the poor in spirit ('Blessed are the poor in spirit', Matt. 5:3; 'Blessed are ye poor', Luke 6:20). As material poverty is to spiritual poverty, so childhood in years is to childhood of soul. The physical state is like a sacrament of the spiritual disposition. Certain natural qualities in the poor and in children are a providential sign of the super-natural virtues of the Christian.[38] Bernanos saw the common factor as a readiness to receive, an openness to gift. The poor in spirit, the childlike in heart, are those who are emptied of self, without defences, unobstructing souls who, like the Lord's lowly Handmaid, let all His glory through. In a gesture typical of his humour and simplicity, Bernanos wrote this eulogy of poverty and childhood in a little girl's autograph album:

Little girls hold out their albums to grown-ups as the poor hold out their hands. And both are usually disappointed, for no one in the universe knows what real disappointment is except the lucky few of the Beatitudes, that is to say, children and the poor ... But you have held out your album to poets. And I believe that poets – miracle of miracles! – have given to you without counting the cost, because poets are by nature lavishly generous. So never forget that this hideous world is kept going by the sweet con-spiracy – eternally resisted, eternally reborn – of the poets and the children. Be loyal to the poets, remain loyal to childhood. Never become a grown-up.[39]

The natural receptivity of the child reveals a mysterious law of the supernatural order: for the soul to give, it first must receive. The Curé of Ambricourt wants to give himself, to abandon himself, totally to God, but there is a kind of poverty

[37] *Lettre aux Anglais*, p. 199.
[38] *Le chrétien Bernanos*, p. 556.
[39] Cited by Balthasar, *Le chrétien Bernanos*, pp. 283f.

even in his generosity. His giving depends on the prior movement of God's and other people's taking:

> Dear God, I give you everything, with a glad heart. The only thing
> is I don't know how to give. I give in the sense of letting people
> take from me. The best thing is to remain calm. I don't know how
> to give, but you know how to take ... And yet I should like, just
> once, to have been superbly generous to you.[40]

'My grace is sufficient for thee', says the God-Man to St Paul,
'for power is made perfect in weakness' (2 Cor. 12:9). The child
in his very defencelessness is strong, for he does not block out
the strengthening gifts poured out upon him. He is therefore
the model of the Catholic Christian, who clings to Mother
Church and receives from her the abundance of graces that flow
from the Heart of her Spouse. As the Curé of Torcy says:

> Childhood and extreme old age ought to be the two great trials of
> man. But it is from that very sense of his own powerlessness that
> the child humbly draws the source of his joy. He leaves everything
> to his mother, don't you see? Past, present, and future, his whole
> life, all life is contained in a glance, and that glance is a smile. You
> know, my boy, if they'd left things to us, the Church would have
> given mankind this kind of supreme security.[41]

The poor little priest of Ambricourt does not resist the empowering action of the Holy Spirit, and so, in his very infirmity,
he can be a good father to his people. After his conversation
with the countess, he writes in his journal:

> Poor priest that I am, in the presence of this woman who is
> superior to me in age, birth, wealth, and intelligence, I realized,
> yes I realized, what fatherhood is.[42]

The Child on the Cross

Just after the Curé of Ambricourt has been told by the doctor
that he is dying, his childhood and youth flood back into his

[40] *Journal*, OR 1245.
[41] *Journal*, OR 1045.
[42] Ibid., 1170.

heart, not with a pang of regret, but with a surge of gratitude and the joy of rediscovery: 'For the first time in years – perhaps for the first time ever – I seem to stand before my youth and look upon it without mistrust. I have rediscovered a forgotten face. And my youth looks back at me and forgives me.'[43] At the moment of truth, as the pretences of adult life fall away, the Risen Christ gives the dying man the chance of regaining the simplicity of childhood. Shortly before his own death in 1948, Bernanos wrote these lines in his diary:

> Just as He sacrifices Himself on each altar where Mass is cele-brated, so He begins again to die in each man in his agony. We will all that He wills, but we do not know that we will it. We do not know ourselves. Sin makes us live on the surface of ourselves. We only go back inside ourselves to die, and there it is that He awaits us.[44]

And, as Albert Béguin said, in death, with and in Christ, is the child that each of us used to be.

> It is there that the Lord awaits us, but there too waits the child of the past, who has patiently stayed in the shadows, free from the lies of superficial life, ready to reappear when the creature will need no more than his child eyes to see what the adult's dull sight has never seen.[45]

Bernanos does not glorify life's beginning to the contempt of life's end. On the contrary, he shows us how the beginning awaits re-discovery in the end. Death, disease, and the slow decline of old age entered this world through the sin of Adam (cf. Rom. 5:12), but by the providence of God they can be an opportunity for a man to recover all that was most beautiful in his childhood: humility, gratitude, receptivity. Even the humiliations of old age (being 'sans everything'), to Christian ears at least, are an echo of the frailties of infancy. Moreover, Bernanos has the marvellous insight that the graces we need for our dying are communicated through the Eucharist. The Sacrifice of the Cross is not locked away in the chronicles of

---

[43] Ibid., 1254.
[44] OR xxv.
[45] *Bernanos par lui-même* (Paris, 1954), p. 12.

history, but is daily re-presented, and its saving power applied anew, in the Sacrifice of the Mass. By offering the divine Victim to the Father, through and with the priest, and by eating His Body and drinking His Blood, we receive from the Holy Spirit the grace to make our living and dying a living and dying to the Lord (cf. Rom. 14:8), the childlike self-surrender of a son-in-the-Son. To share in the simplicity of the Child Christ, we must share in the sufferings of the Crucified Christ – first sacramentally in Baptism and the Eucharist, then by faith and love amidst the terrors of death.

In the *Dialogues*, the Prioress explains that the 'little way' is the path of sacrifice, the road to Calvary:

> What the little shepherd-boy does from time to time, by an impulse of his heart, we have to do day and night. Not that we have any reason to think we pray better than he does; on the contrary, that simplicity of soul, that tender abandonment to the Divine Majesty which in him is an inspiration of the moment, a grace, a kind of illumination of genius, we consecrate our whole lives to acquiring, or to rediscovering it if we have known it, for it is one of the gifts which most often does not survive childhood ... Once out of childhood, we have to suffer for a long time to re-enter it, just as when the night is over, we find another dawn.[46]

The Child as Saint

All of Bernanos's saints are childlike: Donissan, Chevance, Chantal.[47] When he learns that he is going to die young, the Country Priest says: 'There was no old man in me.'[48] But even if he had survived to be ninety, the Curé of Ambricourt would still have been a child, for spiritual childhood is not dated by the calendar. An old man can be young in Christian joy, just as a young man can be old in worldly cynicism.

> Childhood is the true name of youth; what we call the spirit of childhood is the very spirit of youth, and this genius which from

[46] *Dialogues des carmélites*, OR 1586.

[47] See William Bush, *Souffrance et expiation dans la pensée de Georges Bernanos* (Paris, 1962), p. 105.

[48] *Journal*, OR 1254.

age to age makes fruitful and renews history is, strictly speaking, the genius of childhood. The word *youth* is equivocal. Indeed, as we all know, there are young men who, in their ambition, avarice, and deviousness are just like some old crooked provincial lawyer.[49]

Remaining the child I used to be, or becoming a child once again, is a grace from God. It is not a feat of the imagination, nor a matter of self-conscious youthfulness in dress and demeanour – that is the childishness which is the sure sign of an *enfant humilié*. We have to be regenerated into spiritual childhood as a gift from above, by water and the Holy Spirit. We have to be transformed by the rejuvenating grace of the incarnate Son of God. In Baptism, He pours the Spirit of childhood into our hearts, makes us partakers of His Sonship, children in Him of the heavenly Father. And when mortal sin kills our innocence, the grace of the confessional can resurrect it. As the young Curé of Fénouille assures the mad mayor in *Monsieur Ouine*: 'The grace of God makes the most hardened of men a little child.'[50] Absolution, as a second baptism, is a rebirth and return to childhood.[51]

Like every grace, spiritual childhood is not a private possession but a treasure to be shared in the Communion of Saints. In a crisis of agony, the wretched Cénabre realizes that he has been living a lie, and confides in another priest, the saintly Abbé Chevance, who now assumes responsibility for his fate. Chevance has preserved his 'child's soul'.[52] He is a man of simple faith, totally abandoned to God, but, beneath the meekness and apparent timidity, so often mocked by the worldly wise, is 'a boldness in spiritual ways, an extraordinary sense of the grace of God'.[53] In a world ruled by the prince of untruth and pride, he is a scandal, a sign of contradiction. The strength upon which he draws in the struggle for Cénabre's

[49] *Français, si vous saviez* (Paris, 1961), p. 270.
[50] OR 1520.
[51] '"Absolution ... would mean being reborn", he [the mayor] said finally in a strange voice and made his way towards the door' (ibid.).
[52] *L'imposture*, OR 337.
[53] Ibid.

salvation is a 'devastating simplicity'.[54] Cénabre reacts with anger and sarcasm, but Chevance quietly accepts the contempt. As his death approaches, Chevance is increasingly anxious about not having saved Cénabre. The young Chantal de Clergerie sees the good priest's pain. She cannot bear the thought of Chevance dying tortured by anguish, as if he were somehow dying the death of Cénabre. And so, by a mystical substitution, Chantal gives Chevance her joy and takes on herself his fear, his sorrow, and thus his responsibility for the senile soul of Cénabre. Grace flows from Christ the Head to Chantal, and through Chantal to Chevance and Cénabre. He who took on the weight of the whole world's sin enables His members to bear the burden of their brother's weakness. At the very end of *La joie*, Cénabre regains faith through the sacrificial death of the childlike Chantal. His last words are those of a child of God: *Pater noster*.[55]

Bernanos was proud of the childlike saints of his novels, but he loved with tender devotion the childlike saints of the Church, especially the two heroic young Frenchwomen, St Joan of Arc and St Thérèse of Lisieux, whom he regularly and rightly connected.[56] St Joan – a girl of unconquerable faith and courageous charity, condemned by a tribunal of cowardly greybeards – is a symbol of the central struggle of history: 'It is the child in her which is condemned and totally abandoned, tortured more grimly than the little girl for whom Ivan Karamazov denies God and renounces eternal happiness.'[57] As for the Little Flower, Balthasar says that she is 'omnipresent in the works of Bernanos'.[58] Thérèse is the embodiment of that spirit of childhood which he exhorts France and all Christendom to take up as sword and shield. This saint, 'whose stunning career shows the tragically urgent character of the message entrusted to her, invites you to become children again'.[59] She

[54] *La joie*, OR 611.

[55] Ibid., p. 724.

[56] See Guy Gaucher, 'Bernanos et Sainte Thérèse de l'Enfant Jésus', *Études bernanosiennes* 1 (1960), 9.

[57] Balthasar, *Le chrétien Bernanos*, p. 291. See Bernanos, *Jeanne relapse et sainte* (Paris, 1934).

[58] *Le chrétien Bernanos*, p. 289.

[59] *Grands cimetières*, p. 269.

proves that humble self-abandonment to God is the wellspring of fortitude and the only true honour. The Chantal of *La joie* is modelled on Thérèse,[60] while the Curé of Ambricourt is one of Thérèse's little brothers, a comrade of the real-life Bellière and Roulland. Balthasar describes the *Journal* as 'a kind of adaptation in depth of the Thérèsian message ... a free transposition of its central intuitions, raised up from the earthly level to the spiritual'.[61] The Curé's death is a 'little death, as little as possible', and his dying words are a direct quotation from the *novissima verba* of the Little Flower: 'All is grace.'[62]

Once we recognize sanctity as the 'spirit of childhood', we can appreciate why, in Bernanos's novels, sin is always the sin against childhood, why Satan and his human co-operators are the enemies of childhood's simplicity. 'The simplicity of God, the terrible simplicity of God, which damned the pride of the angels.'[63] The sin of the fallen angels was the sin of pride. They sinned by desiring to be as God, not by making themselves equal to God (they knew that was impossible), but by desiring as their final happiness something that they could achieve by their own natural powers. They turned their backs on the supernatural bliss which depends on the fatherly liberality of grace.[64] Their sin was, therefore, an act of high-and-mightiness, the refusal of childlike dependence. Into that refusal they enticed Adam, and towards that refusal they still tempt the sons

[60] For the correspondences between Chantal and Thérèse, see Gaucher, art. cit., 24ff. William Bush offers this comment: '[St Thérèse's] *Story of a Soul* was thus, through Bernanos, to pass into the realm of the French novel, and Chantal de Clergerie, the heroine of *Joy* who redeems the impostor priest Cénabre, is Bernanos' attempt at incarnating Thérèse's spirituality' (*Georges Bernanos* [New York, 1969], p. 79).

[61] *Le chrétien Bernanos*, p. 289.

[62] *Journal*, OR 1259. On 5 June 1897 Thérèse gave Mother Agnès this disconcerting consolation: 'Don't worry if you find me dead one morning. It will simply be because Papa the good God has come to look for me. It is doubtless a great grace to receive the Sacraments, but when the good God does not permit it, it's still all right ... *All is grace*' (OC 1009). Bernanos was amused that people thought he had coined this aphorism. When he was dying, he asked the priest who visited him each day: 'Are you another one of these people who think I said "All is grace"?' (G. Gaucher, art. cit., 5).

[63] *Journal*, OR 1192.

[64] Cf. St Thomas Aquinas, *Summa theologiae*, 1a 63, 3.

and daughters of Adam. As pure spirits, the fallen angels are ageless, but if humble obedience to God is spiritual youth, their rebellious pride is decrepitude.

The Youngest Sister

Behind Thérèse and Joan stands another young maiden, the human person who embodies the spirit of childhood with immaculate perfection:

> Thérèse and Joan are like the exterior, accessible bastions of an unapproachable citadel. Bernanos's love of the Virgin Mary was too deep, too tender, for him to hang it up on every corner of his work. He mentioned her only once, because without her he could not survive; just once he brings her out from her invisible and permanent presence to place her in the full light.[65]

Our Lady makes her appearance at the end of the Curé's long and painful path, at the precise moment when everything is beginning to fall apart. His friend, the Curé of Torcy, tells him that he must not fail to pray to the angels and to the Mother of God:

> The eyes of Our Lady are the only real child eyes that have ever been raised to our shame and sadness. Yes, lad, to pray to her properly, you have to feel those eyes of hers upon you. They are not eyes of indulgence – for there is no indulgence without some kind of bitter experience. No, they are eyes of tender compassion, sorrowful surprise, and with something more in them, something inconceivable, inexpressible, something which makes her younger than sin, younger than the race from which she sprang, and though a mother, by grace Mother of All Graces, the youngest sister of the human race.[66]

The eternal Son, true God from true God, became true man in the Virgin's womb in order, by His Cross and Resurrection, to make all things new, to regenerate a world worn out and wearied by sin and death. In her Immaculate Conception, Our Lady received by anticipation the rejuvenating grace of her Son.

[65] Balthasar, *Le chrétien Bernanos*, pp. 292f.
[66] *Journal*, OR 1194.

In her flesh she was a true daughter of Adam, but her soul was preserved from ever feeling the greying touch of his sin. She alone among human persons never lost the innocence of her infancy. By the grace of the Holy Spirit who indwells her soul from her conception, the Blessed Virgin's assent to God's will is freed from the tired old cynicism, the mouldering mistrust of the sinner. In her Yes to God, she is inextinguishably child-like, and now, glorified in body as well as in soul, she enjoys the eternal youth of her Son's Resurrection. It is to Mary Immaculate, younger than sin and therefore closer to sinners than sinners can ever be to themselves, that the Country Priest looks in his agony, as he enters his night. Bernanos's 'spirit of childhood' is more than just a spirit, a sentiment, a thought; it is a young girl of flesh and blood, the Ever-Virgin Mother of God.

Bernanos and Chesterton: True to the Child

Maisie Ward said that comparing Léon Bloy to Chesterton was like comparing Francis Thompson to Shakespeare: there is an embarrassment of disproportion.[67] Comparing Bernanos with Chesterton is less far-fetched, like comparing Corneille to Shakespeare. Bernanos had a Chestertonian quality which Maisie Ward claimed Bloy lacked – a tremendous sense of humour. For all the anguish of his novels, despite the pains and disappointments of his life, Bernanos had the virtue of *hilaritas*, which he exercised as much at his own as at others' expense. In Béguin's *Bernanos par lui-même*, there is a cartoon which lacks the artistry of Chesterton but has all his self-mockery. It shows Bernanos asleep, head on arms, at a café table, with a half-drunk wine bottle beside him. The caption is: 'The illustrious author hard at work.' Even better are the words scribbled on a photograph taken in Rio during the war: 'Oh no, I look like Claudel!' More important still, though, is the convergence in the thinking of these two very different men on the subject of childhood.

Chesterton was 'true to the child he used to be'. On the way to his wedding, he stopped at the dairy where he had always

---

[67] Ward, *Return*, p. 9.

drunk a glass of milk when walking with his mother as a child; it was, he said, 'a fitting ceremonial to unite the two great relations of a man's life'.[68] He was gathering up his childhood and taking it into his marriage. Gilbert wanted to give his whole self to Frances, even the boy he used to be. He was convinced that childhood is not a dull track towards the bold highway of adulthood. It is itself already 'the white and solid road and the worthy beginning of the life of man'.[69] In the shadow of death, Chesterton still walked in the sunshine of his childhood. His end somehow contained his beginning.[70]

Like Bernanos, Chesterton believed that the child is the guardian of truth. There is, he says, a deluded view of 'mature persons, who have themselves lost much of their sense of reality ... that a child is concerned only with make-believe'.[71] Even Robert Louis Stevenson, whom he otherwise so heartily admired, made the mistake of thinking that the child lives 'in a dazed day-dream, in which he cannot distinguish fancy from fact'.[72] No, said Chesterton, 'the real child does not confuse fact and fiction. He simply likes fiction ... No possible amount of playing at robbers would ever bring him an inch nearer to thinking it is really right to rob'.[73] The child is a realist in the strict metaphysical sense. His wonder is an amazement at what is there:

> Mine is a memory of a sort of white light on everything, cutting things out very clearly, and rather emphasizing their solidity. The point is that the white light had a sort of wonder in it, as if the world were as new as myself; but not that the world was anything but a real world. I am much more disposed *now* to fancy that an apple-tree in the moonlight is some sort of ghost or grey nymph ... But when I was a child I had a sort of confident astonishment in contemplating the apple-tree as an apple-tree.[74]

[68] Chesterton, *Autobiography*, p. 30.
[69] Ibid., p. 49.
[70] 'But for me my end is my beginning, as Maurice Baring quoted of Mary Stuart' (ibid., p. 355).
[71] Ibid., p. 39.
[72] Ibid., p. 42.
[73] Ibid., p. 39.
[74] Ibid., pp. 42f.

The child has a keen 'appetite for things as they actually are, and because they actually are; for a stone because it is a stone, or a story because it is a story'.[75] What Bernanos called *imposture*, the deceiving of self and others through the passing off of fancy as fact, is the sin of the devious adult. 'It is only the grown man who lives a life of make-believe and pretending; and it is he who has his head in a cloud.'[76]

Chesterton shares Bernanos's (and Péguy's) view that the characteristic sin of the modern world is hostility to childhood. For him, this antagonism reached its most extreme form in the evil of Birth Control, or 'Birth Prevention', as he insisted on calling it. In the contraceptive mind, he argued, the child is seen not as a person, the fruit of love and the gift of God, but as a horrible thing to be prevented, a disaster to be averted. But children are only things for those who live for things:

> [M]y contempt boils over into bad behaviour when I hear the common suggestion that a birth is avoided because people want to be 'free' to go to the cinema or buy a gramophone or a loudspeaker. What makes me want to walk over such people like doormats is that they use the word 'free'. By every act of that sort they chain themselves to the most servile and mechanical system yet tolerated by men ... For a child is the very sign and sacrament of personal freedom. He is a fresh free will added to the wills of the world; he is something that his parents have freely chosen to produce and which they freely agree to protect ... He has been born without the intervention of any master or lord. He is a creation and a contribution; he is their own creative contribution to creation ... People who prefer the mechanical pleasures to such a miracle are jaded and enslaved. They are preferring the last, crooked, indirect, borrowed, repeated and exhausted things of our dying Capitalist civilisation, to the reality which is the only rejuvenation of all civilisation. It is they who are hugging the chains of their old slavery; it is the child who is ready for the new world.[77]

[75] *Chaucer* (New York, 1932), p. 167.
[76] Ibid., p. 54.
[77] *The Well and the Shallows*, in *The Collected Works of G. K. Chesterton*, vol. 3, pp. 440f.

Chesterton saw, with a kind of passion of precision, that once marriage is cut off from the family, whenever lust triumphs over life, society, however rich in technical accomplishment, will be a sterile slave to the 'demons of old age'. The world that hates children is the ante-chamber of Hell.

It is above all in their understanding of Christmas, in their love of the 'God in the Cave and His Virgin Mother ('the woman made for morning when the stars were young'), that the minds and hearts of these two Christian knights come closest. Chesterton saw that the external grace of Christmas could bring with it the internal grace of conversion. Through the memory of Christmas Past even the most hardened unbeliever might find the Infant God, or rather, through Christmas Past, the Infant Child could seek and save the unbeliever and lead him to the Christmas Everlasting of Heaven.

Any agnostic or atheist whose childhood has ever known a real Christmas has ever afterwards, whether he likes it or not, an association in his mind between two ideas that most of mankind must regard as remote from each other: the idea of a baby and the idea of an unknown strength that sustains the stars.[78]

Since the death of Chesterton in 1936 and of Bernanos in 1948, the world has seen horrors perpetrated against childhood without parallel in human history. In war and in peace, innocent little ones have been made a direct object of attack. In a whole climate of feeling and thought, the child has become a problem to be prevented, an enemy to be destroyed, a product to be manufactured, an object of experimentation, a commodity to be sold, even an instrument of loathsome pleasure. When a man of good will hears of these atrocities, he instinctively calls them 'diabolical'. His instinct is right. These evils are the work of men, and nothing can lessen their responsibility for them; but behind them all lie the superhuman schemings of the Devil, that fallen created spirit who is human nature's vengeful adversary, the implacable foe of innocence and simplicity. But there is hope, there is a Morning Star which came back from the

---

[78] *The Everlasting Man*, in *The Collected Works of G. K. Chesterton*, vol. 2, p. 302.

dead and never sets. The Seed of the Woman has crushed the Serpent. I cannot again be the child I used to be, but the Lamb of God can make me like the Child that He is for ever, the Only-Begotten in the bosom of the Father.

> Have a myriad children been quickened,
> Have a myriad children grown old,
> Grown gross and unloved and embittered,
> Grown cunning and savage and cold?
> God abides in a terrible patience,
> Unangered, unworn,
> And again for the child that was squandered
> A child is born.[79]

---

[79] Chesterton, 'The Nativity', Mackey, p. 139.

4

Like Mother, Like Sons

Balthasar, Chesterton, and the Way of the Lamb

The discovery of the differences is easy; the challenge is to reveal some resemblances. Hans Urs von Balthasar and Gilbert Keith Chesterton were separated by time and place. H.U. was born into a Catholic family in Lucerne in the year that the still Anglican G.K. published *Heretics* in London. When the (by then) Catholic layman died, the young Jesuit was still studying for the priesthood. The two never met. It is unlikely that Chesterton ever read any of the articles that Balthasar had written before 1936. Judging from the remark in *Tremendous Trifles* to the effect that the Swiss 'have produced no art or literature at all, and are by far the most mundane, sensible, and business-like people in Europe',[1] I suspect that Chesterton was not a regular reader of the *Schweizerische Rundschau*, in which most of these remarkable essays – on 'The Catholic Religion and Art', 'The Art of Fugue', and 'The Metaphysics of Erich Przyrwara' – first appeared.

The differences between our two protagonists are so vast and obvious that the task of comparing them may seem vain and foolish. However, as Chesterton once reminded H. G. Wells, 'the fact of two things being different implies that they are similar'.[2] The unlikenesses between Balthasar and Chesterton are great, and yet, as I hope to show, the likenesses are even greater. They followed the Lamb to the house of the Father, in the Holy

[1] G. K. Chesterton, *Tremendous Trifles* (New York, 1955), pp. 93f.
[2] G. K. Chesterton, *Heretics* (New York, 1906), p. 82.

Spirit of baptismal childhood. There is a deep mystery about these two figures of the recent past: though ancient, they appear daily more youthful, ever more appealing to the men of our time. As the years lengthen since their death, their fame rises, and their wisdom shines ever more splendidly. If there is to be a renewal of Christian culture, then these two may hold the seeds of Spring.

To draw out the likenesses, I shall first discuss Balthasar's explicit references to Chesterton, and then, to adapt something St Augustine said about the two Testaments of Scripture,[3] I shall give examples of how Balthasar lies hidden in Chesterton and Chesterton becomes clear in Balthasar.

I. Balthasar on Chesterton

1. Chesterton and the Tradition

Balthasar helps us determine Chesterton's proper place in the tradition of Christendom. I can think of no one better equipped to make such a judgement. Balthasar's mentor, the late Cardinal de Lubac, described him as 'the most cultured man of our time'.[4] The range of his knowledge and writing is breathtaking. In the first part of the third volume of his great work *Herrlichkeit*, he opens up, with rigorous detail as well as broad sweep, all the philosophy and literature of the West from Homer and the pre-Socratics to Hölderlin, Hegel, and beyond. He is the critical historian of post-Enlightenment German literature and philosophy,[5] the expositor of the Fathers (his *Kosmische Liturgie* opened a new chapter in the study of St Maximus the Confessor), the theological interpreter of the lives of the saints (St Thérèse of Lisieux and Blessed Elizabeth of Dijon) and of the great Christian writers (Péguy, Bernanos, Claudel, Schneider). He wrote commentaries on Pauline

---

[3] St Augustine said that 'the New [Testament] is hidden in the Old and the Old made manifest in the New' (*Quaestiones in Heptateuchum* 2, 73; PL 34. 623).

[4] Henri de Lubac, 'Un témoin du Christ: Hans Urs von Balthasar', *Civitas* 20 (1965), 588.

[5] See Balthasar, *Apokalypse der deutschen Seele* (Heidelberg and Salzburg, 1937–1939).

epistles and part of the *Summa Theologiae* of St Thomas. He
conversed with Barth the Protestant and Buber the Jew. He
constructed a theological trilogy based on the transcendentals
of beauty, goodness, and truth. And all this learning, this
unabated energy in reading and writing, was dedicated, not
to advancement within the academy, but to the unfolding of
Divine Revelation in the Church. Balthasar, true servant of
the Tradition, had, among moderns, an unrivalled mastery of
the Tradition.

Balthasar is well qualified, then, to make a judgement on
where Chesterton stands in the history of Christianity. He
regards him as one of the great men of the Catholic Tradition,
to be mentioned without hyperbole in the same breath as
Augustine or Thomas. In the second volume of *Herrlichkeit*, he
explains why he has chosen certain theologians and not others
as examples of what he calls the 'Theological Aesthetic', theologies centred on the revealed beauty (or glory) of God.
Between Irenaeus and Augustine, a discussion of divine beauty
in Origen and Gregory of Nyssa would have been in order.
After Dante, Ramon Lull and Nicholas of Cusa might have
been brought into the picture. And alongside Gerard Manley
Hopkins, he could have presented two other Englishmen who
perceived the beauty of God revealed in Christ: John Henry
Newman and Gilbert Keith Chesterton.[6]

In the end, Balthasar did not choose Chesterton as a repre-
sentative of the Theological Aesthetic, but it is enough for us
to know that he was on the short-list. In Balthasar's mind,
Chesterton is a master in Israel. Like Dante and the other writers
in the third volume of *Herrlichkeit*, he is an example of what
Balthasar calls the 'lay style' in Catholic theology. After (but not
because of) St Thomas Aquinas, argues Balthasar, there is a sad
narrowing of theology in the Latin Church. The exalted science
which St Thomas called *sacra doctrina* settles down prosaically
to being a course of study for the clergy or a dry academic
speciality. It is left to the laymen, such as Dante, Péguy, and
Chesterton, or to priests working outside of the schools, such as

---

[6] Balthasar, *Herrlichkeit. Eine theologische Ästhetik*, vol. 2, Fächer der Stile, part
1, Klerikale Stile (Einsiedeln, 1962), p. 18.

St John of the Cross, Cardinal Newman, and Hopkins, to keep alive wonder and a sense of beauty in the *intellectus fidei*.[7]

It may come as a shock to discover that Balthasar, the most cultured man of our time, thought of Chesterton as a theologian, the working journalist who lacked even a first degree. Indeed, to the self-consciously grown-up world of professional university theology, Balthasar himself, who had no doctorate in theology and never held a chair, may seem amateurish. And indeed, in a sense, he was. In the first volume of *Herrlichkeit*, he points out that, when 'measured by today's scientific ideals, nearly all the great and historically influential Christian theologies have been dilettantish, fashioned as they were by "amateurs" and "enthusiasts" for the Word of God'.[8] Balthasar is thinking of that note of sheer rhapsody, of boyish delight in the riches of Divine Revelation, which runs through the writings of the Fathers and is not lost by the greatest of the Schoolmen. This is the glorious, not scandalous, amateurishness of Chesterton and of Balthasar himself.

2. The Good Humour of Hope

Chesterton makes brief appearances both in *Herrlichkeit*, which contemplates Divine Revelation as the manifestation in Christ of the Trinity's beauty or glory, and in *Theodramatik*, which considers Divine Revelation as the drama of the Trinity's self-giving goodness. In both places, Chesterton – the man and the work – is praised as an apostle of evangelical good humour, of the humour of Christian hope. In the third volume of *Herrlichkeit*, when he is expounding 'The Metaphysics of the Saints', that is to say, what the lives of the saints reveal to us of the beauty of being, Balthasar places Chesterton in the company of those Christian writers, such as Wolfram, Cervantes, and Dostoyevsky, who have found spiritual beauty even in folly, the folly of the fools for Christ's sake.[9] Chesterton would be honoured to join this motley crew, this crew in motley: 'A man who has faith', he says in *Heretics*, 'must be prepared not only to be a martyr, but to be a fool. It is absurd to say that a man is

[7] Ibid., p. 13.
[8] Ibid., vol. 1, Schau der Gestalt (Einsiedeln, 1961), p. 72.
[9] Ibid., vol. 3/1, Im Raum der Metaphysik (Einsiedeln, 1965), p. 94.

ready to toil and die for his convictions when he is not even
ready to wear a wreath round his head for them'.[10]

Balthasar finds in Chesterton confirmation for his belief that
humour is an essential attribute of the Catholic religion and a
quality to be found in its great saints. According to St Thomas
Aquinas, a sense of humour is part of the virtue of modesty. He
called it 'cheerfulness' (*iucunditas*) or 'good conversation' (*bona
conversatio*) and identified it with the Aristotelian virtue of
eutrapelia or 'ready wit'.[11] Now, in addition to this natural sense
of humour, which may be greater or less in a man according to
temperament and culture, there is a supernatural sense of
humour made possible by grace and charity and the Gifts of
the Holy Spirit. This is the rich and full-bodied joy, that 'gigantic
secret of the Christian',[12] which we see in the saints. Walter
Hilton and St Thomas More gave it the good old English name
of 'mirth' and expressed their hope that they would enjoy it in
Heaven.[13] Sometimes this holy mirth presupposes and builds
on the saints' natural cheerfulness. At other times, it overcomes
and heals their natural melancholy. In either case, it is shining
proof that, by divinizing us, the grace of the God-Man makes
us more deeply and richly human. Balthasar writes:

> The saints are never killjoy maiden aunts, professional fault
> finders, in other words, people who have no sense of humour ...
> We can use this word "humour" to denote a mysterious and
> unmistakable charism inseparable from the Catholic faith.[14]

[10] Op. cit., p. 97.

[11] Cf. *Summa Theologiae*, 168, 2, *sed contra*.

[12] Cf. Chesterton, *Orthodoxy*, p. 298.

[13] In the heavenly Jerusalem, says Hilton in his translation of the *Stimulus
Amoris*, 'shall we joy and have mirth, each man of other's joy as of his own,
and sovereignly we shall have joy of the unmeasurable mickleness of God's
nature and of His wisdom and of His goodness' (edited by C. Kirchberger
under the title *The Goad of Love* [London, 1952], pp. 212f.). In his last letter to
his daughter Meg, More wrote: 'Farewell, my dear child, and pray for me, and
I shall for you and all your friends, that we may merrily meet in Heaven' (*The
Correspondence of Sir Thomas More*, edited by E. F. Rogers [Princeton, 1947], p.
64). According to St Thomas Aquinas, *iucunditas* will fill the souls of the blessed
and, after the resurrection, their bodies also (cf. *Commentum in Quartum Librum
Sententiarum*, dist. 44, q. 1, a. 3, qa. 4, obj. 4).

[14] Balthasar, *Der antirömische Affekt. Wie lässt sich das Papsttum in der
Gesamtkirche integrieren* (Freiburg, 1974), p. 250.

Balthasar contrasts the saints' cheerful love of the Church with the criticisms levelled against her by 'the moaners, savage satirists, grumblers, carping critics, full of bitter scorn, know-alls who think they have the monopoly of infallible judgement'.[15] He makes this point in a book with the title *Der antirömische Affekt*, 'The Anti-Roman Complex', which expounds the theology of the Papacy against the background of hatred of the Papacy, not just outside but inside the Catholic Church. The good-humoured saints are content with the teaching office that comes from Christ; the sobre-sided critics are loyal only to the magisterium of their own minds. The saints love the Church – the historical, visible Roman Catholic Church, not just some ideal Church – because, for all the blemishes of her earthly form, she is the beloved Bride of Christ, teaching His truth and communicating His grace. The shortcomings of the clergy do not depress them; it simply drives them to more fervent prayer and penance. They strike their own, not their brothers', breasts. They find light and comfort in the dogmatic truth defended by St Augustine against the Donatists and summed up so well by Cardinal Charles Journet: the Church is without sin, but not without sinners.[16]

A book still waits to be written, says Balthasar, on the humour of the saints.

> Goethe has given us a short chapter of it in his *Philip Neri, the Humorous Saint* ... But what merriment do we find as early as Irenaeus, when he pricks the shimmering bubbles of the cosmic systems of Gnosticism ... What a boyish spirit of adventure there is in Bonaventure's *Itinerarium*! What flashes of humour in Ignatius Loyola and Teresa of Avila (you look for them in vain in the solemn Reformers)! And nearer our own time what charming mischief in little Thérèse, to say nothing of Claudel's homely laughter (through tears of passion). What lighthearted *grandezza* in Péguy as he opens his Christian soul to all the values of paganism and Judaism, only to lay down all these treasures, with a smile, at the Christmas Crib.[17]

---

[15] Ibid.

[16] Charles Journet, *L'Église du Verbe incarné*, vol. 2, Sa structure interne et son unité catholique, second edition (Paris, 1962), pp. 904ff.

[17] Balthasar, *Der antirömische Affekt*, p. 252.

The passing reference to St Ignatius Loyola deserves to be expanded. In *Herrlichkeit*, Balthasar, the former Jesuit, shows his abiding devotion to the one he always called *Sanctus Pater Noster* when he commends the humour and 'wise patience' of St Ignatius' love of the Church. He notes the contrast with 'the impatience of Luther's Reformation with its violent attack on dogmas, structures, and images'. In an age of fierce controversy and religious war, the founder of the Jesuits will not criticize the Church; he has only words of praise for the means of grace she offers mankind. Balthasar suggests that Ignatius would have enjoyed singing the old negro spiritual: 'Give me that old time religion, it's good enough for me!'[18]

Into this heroic legion of Christian laughter Balthasar drafts Chesterton.

> And there is most decidedly humour in the way Chesterton, the defender of 'nonsense, humility, penny dreadfuls, and other despised things', responds to the bestial seriousness and desperate optimism of modern world views – which are united in their opposition to Rome – with the statement that only in Catholic form can one preserve the wonder of being, liberty, childlikeness, the adventure, the resilient, energizing paradox of existence.[19]

It is significant that Balthasar quotes Chesterton's *Orthodoxy* twice in his book on the meaning of Catholicity, *Katholisch*. Humour is a defining mark of the Catholic. This has sometimes been ruefully recognized by Protestants. First in *Der antirömische Affekt* and then again in *Katholisch*, Balthasar describes how poor Kierkegaard used to look 'wistfully beyond the limits of his melancholy religion towards the Catholic paradise where, for all its seriousness, a person can be "a little mischievous", where "all that is childlike recurs in a heightened form, as a mature naïveté, simplicity, wonder, humour"'.[20]

[18] *Herrlichkeit*, vol. 3/1, Im Raum der Metaphysik (Einsiedeln, 1965), pp. 462f.
[19] Ibid., p. 251. Balthasar mentions another Englishman who belongs within the Christian good humour tradition: 'And, with a good conscience, I take the liberty of appropriating for the Catholic Tradition the humour of C. S. Lewis (whose tales are more beautiful than Brentano's)' (ibid., p. 252).
[20] Ibid. Kierkegaard's sense of the good humour of Catholicism is also mentioned by Balthasar in *Katholisch. Aspekte des Mysteriums* (Einsiedeln, 1975), p. 40. Chesterton was once reprimanded by his atheistic adversary, Joseph

But what is this grace of humour that so brightens the faces of the saints? Balthasar and Chesterton provide a definition that is philosophical and theological rather than merely psychological.

First, the humour of the saints is the humour of *humility*. A man who has surrendered himself with Christ to the Father, in the wild abandon of faith and charity, cannot take himself seriously. We can see this in the case of St Paul. The two Epistles to the Corinthians, particularly the closing chapters of the second, are a riot of self-mockery: 'If I must boast, I will boast of the things that show my weakness ... I must boast; there is nothing to be gained by it, but I will go on to visions and revelations of the Lord ... I have been a fool!' (2 Cor. 11:30; 12:1, 11). The Apostle can laugh at himself because it is Christ, not his self, that is his centre of gravity: 'It is no longer I who live, but Christ who lives in me' (Gal. 2:20). St Paul is a happy man because he knows that even his most humiliating weaknesses, once offered up, can be transfigured by grace: 'My grace is sufficient for you, for my power is made perfect in weakness' (2 Cor. 12:9).

The example of St Paul is my own thought, but the reasoning is Balthasar's and Chesterton's. In *Der antirömische Affekt* Balthasar quotes the passage in *Orthodoxy* where Chesterton says that pride is heavy in its hold, while humility is light in its touch:

> Angels can fly because they can take themselves lightly. This has been always the instinct of Christendom ... pride is the downward drag of all things into an easy solemnity. One 'settles down' into a sort of selfish seriousness; but one has to rise to a gay self-forgetfulness ... It is much easier to write a good *Times* leading article than a good joke in *Punch*. For solemnity flows out of men naturally; but laughter is a leap. It is easy to be heavy; hard to be light. Satan fell by the force of gravity.[21]

McCabe, for bringing humour into their debates. Chesterton replied that McCabe 'ought himself to be importing humour into every controversy; for unless a man is in part a humorist, he is only in part a man' (*Heretics*, p. 233).

[21] Cited in Balthasar, *Der antirömische Affekt*, p. 251. Cf. *Katholisch*, pp. 39f.

The proud man is too weighed down with self-importance to be humorous. In his own sad mind, he has displaced God as the support of the universe, and each day he has the gloomy task of putting the world on his shoulders. But the saint, in imitation of the self-emptying Son, is unencumbered by self-concern, and so he can fly with the merry angels of God.

The second thing to say about the good humour of Catholicism is that it is the good humour of *hope*. For both Balthasar and Chesterton, the enemy is always pessimism. They are united in their diagnosis of late Victorian despair and in their determination to fight its abiding effects in our culture. In the three-volume *Apokalypse der deutschen Seele*, Balthasar gives a more exact description of the 'Prussian' pessimism mentioned in earlier chapters of this book. He charts the development of German thought from the 'Promethean' enthusiasm of early nineteenth-century Idealists to 'The Divinization of Death' in the early twentieth century. In a powerful passage in *Herrlichkeit*, he shows how Schopenhauer, Hegel's 'dark shadow', transforms the 'light-filled and beautiful world of the "ideas"' into the mere 'manifestation of a dark and blind will and thus a perverse and paradoxical place where being denies itself and falls back into nothingness'. It is what Balthasar calls 'Schopenhauer's perfumed nihilism of the salon' which, in their different ways, Wagner, Nietzsche, and Thomas Mann will develop in Germany, and in England George Bernard Shaw. Balthasar says that he agrees with Chesterton's view that Shaw, the 'Irish puritan', turns Schopenhauer 'on his head' by his affirmation of the 'man-trap' of human life.[22]

Balthasar and Chesterton have a common tactic in their Christian war against pessimism. Their first line of attack is metaphysics. The naïve pessimist and the natural optimist, for all their temperamental differences, make the same philosophical mistake: they both imagine that they can step outside of existence and look upon it as a house-hunter would a suite of apartments.

A man belongs to this world before he begins to ask if it is nice to belong to it. He has fought for the flag, and often won heroic

---

[22] *Theodramatik*, vol. 1, Prolegomena (Einsiedeln, 1973), p. 217.

victories for the flag before he has ever enlisted ... My acceptance
of the world is not optimism, it is more like patriotism. It is a
matter of primary loyalty ... The evil of pessimist is, then, not
that he chastises gods and men, but that he does not love what he
chastises – he has not this primary and supernatural loyalty to
things.[23]

In similar fashion, as I shall try to show below, Balthasar
proves that the 'Prussian pessimists' make the mistake of
forgetting that being in its loveliness precedes the ugliness of
their scepticism, as their childhood's wonder comes before
their adulthood's despair. In a word, for both Balthasar and
Chesterton, the unreasonableness of pessimism was proved by
what one might call the prevenient grace of life.

The good-humoured hope of Balthasar and Chesterton is not
a shallow natural optimism, but rather a profound supernatural
optimism, the infused virtue of hope, the optimism of the
redeemed. For them, as for St Thomas Aquinas, Christian hope
is a *theological* virtue, hope in God.[24] It is not for some vaguely
defined happiness that they hope, but for eternal happiness
with Our Lady and the angels and saints in the vision of the
Triune God.[25]

False optimism tries to prove that man fits into the world:
this is the only life man has, and so he has to make the best of it.
By contrast, says Chesterton, 'Christian optimism is based on
the fact that we do *not* fit into the world'.[26] The hope for a final
resting-place in Heaven does not make this world seem
monotonous and stale; on the contrary, it makes it all the more
marvellous and strange. Chesterton continues:

The optimist's pleasure was prosaic, for it dwelt on the
naturalness of everything; the Christian pleasure was poetic, for
it dwelt on the unnaturalness of everything in the light of the
supernatural. The modern philosopher had told me again and
again that I was in the right place, and I had still felt depressed
even in acquiescence. But I had heard that I was in the *wrong*

[23] Chesterton, *Orthodoxy*, pp. 120ff.
[24] Cf. St Thomas Aquinas, *Summa Theologiae*, 2a2ae 17, 5.
[25] Ibid., 17, 2.
[26] Chesterton, *Orthodoxy*, p. 146.

place, and my soul sang for joy, like a bird in Spring. The knowledge found out and illuminated forgotten chambers in the dark house of infancy. I knew now why grass had always seemed to me as queer as the green beard of a giant, and why I could feel homesick at home.[27]

Here Chesterton gives the complete answer to Leibniz, who argued that God was obliged to create our world as the best of all possible worlds. He develops the argument further when he is defending the measured Christian optimism of Dickens:

The world is not to be justified by the mechanical optimists; it is not to be justified as the best of all possible worlds. Its merit is not that it is orderly and explicable; its merit is that it is wild and utterly unexplained. Its merit is precisely that none of us could have conceived such a thing, that we should have rejected the bare idea of it as miracle and unreason. It is the best of all impossible worlds.[28]

The divine and supernatural character of hope and the other Theological Virtues is shown by the fact that all three are paradoxical.[29] They do not go against reason, but they do perceive possibilities to which reason by its own light is blind. That is why Abraham is said to 'hope against hope' (cf. Rom. 4:18); even when there was nothing naturally to be expected, he placed his trust in God. As Chesterton says:

Hope means hoping when things are hopeless, or it is no virtue at all ... The virtue of hope exists only in earthquake and eclipse.[30]

Balthasar shares the audacity of Chesterton's hope. One of his last books bore the title *Was dürfen wir hoffen?*, which could be translated as 'How far can we go in hoping?' The book bristles with difficulties, and I must state candidly that I do not agree with its chief thesis, namely, that Hell is only ever presented by Christ and His Church as a possibility for any of

---

[27] Ibid., pp. 146f.

[28] *Charles Dickens*, new edition (New York, 1942), p. 192.

[29] Chesterton writes: 'They are all three paradoxical, they are all three practical, and they are all three paradoxical because they are practical' (*Heretics*, p. 161).

[30] Ibid., pp. 158f.

the living rather than an actuality for some of the dead.[31] However, one can extract from the book three theses of un-exceptionable orthodoxy which illustrate perfectly what I mean by the audacity of Balthasar's – and Chesterton's – Christian hope. First, he defends St Thomas' teaching that, when they are united in the friendship of charity, one man can hope for the eternal salvation of another.[32] Secondly, we must never give up hope and prayer for the salvation of even the most apparently hardened sinner while he is still living. To do so would be to surrender to the fatalism of Calvinism and Jansenism. St Thérèse's rescue of the soul of the murderer Pranzini is a splendid example of this dauntless trust in the Hound of Heaven. Thirdly, since the Church has not declared officially that any particular human soul is in Hell, of none of the dead should we abandon hope, and so we may properly pray even for the apparently unrepentant in the hope that his soul is detained temporarily in Purgatory rather than eternally in Hell.

The ground of Balthasar's and Chesterton's daring hope in God is the Incarnation, Death, and Resurrection of the Son of God, the great mysteries of joy, sorrow, and glory, which these two men both understand with the full rigour of Chalcedonian orthodoxy. 'Christian hope', says Balthasar, 'can be described as a "better" hope, because it rests on an already accomplished fact, the Resurrection of Christ'.[33] We can hope against hope because all the woes that make us feel hopeless, all our desolating pains in body and mind, have been borne and in principle transfigured by God-made-man. We do not have to worry about the worst befalling us, because the very worst has already happened to the incarnate Son, and He has worsted the worst. We need not fear abandonment because God has been forsaken by God, and there is no Godforsakenness greater; now all the lonelinesses of men are spanned by the arms of the Father's Son and closed in the Spirit of love. As Our Lady says in 'The Ballad of the White Horse', 'the men signed of the sign

---

[31] See the critique of Balthasar's position in Germain Grisez, *The Way of the Lord Jesus*, vol. 3, Difficult Moral Questions (Quincy, 1997), pp. 21–28.

[32] Cf. Balthasar, *Was dürfen wir hoffen?* (Einsiedeln, 1986), ch. 2, passim. Cf. St Thomas Aquinas, *Summa Theologiae*, 2a2ae 20, 17, 3.

[33] Balthasar, *Theodramatik*, vol. 4, Das Endspiel (Einsiedeln, 1983), pp. 125f.

of Christ / Go gaily in the dark'.[34] Even the falling into dust of
our bodies cannot shake us, because in the very Body He took
from the Virgin the divine Word has risen from the tomb,
trampling on death, and through that glorious Body, with
which He feeds us at the altar, He will raise up our lowly bodies
on the last day.

The cry of dereliction stands at the centre of Chesterton's
theology of the Cross, as it does also in Balthasar's. In *The
Everlasting Man*, Chesterton writes:

> There were solitudes beyond where none shall follow. There were
> secrets in the inmost and invisible part of that drama that have no
> symbol in speech; or in any severance of a man from men. Nor is
> it easy for any words less stark and singleminded than those of
> the naked narrative even to hint at the horror of exaltation that
> lifted itself above the hill. Endless expositions have not come to
> the end of it, or even to the beginning. And if there be any sound
> that can produce a silence, we may surely be silent about the end
> and the extremity; when a cry was driven out of that darkness in
> words dreadfully distinct and dreadfully unintelligible, which
> man shall never understand in all the eternity they have
> purchased for him; and for one annihilating instant an abyss that
> is not for our thoughts had opened even in the unity of the
> absolute; and God had been forsaken of God.[35]

Similarly, Balthasar draws from the great cry from the Cross his
own message of hope:

> Only the Christian can look death and its terribleness in the face –
> no death will ever be as terrible as the death of Christ – and in so
> doing not abandon hope for mankind (and for himself in
> mankind), because the whole disaster of death is upheld and
> overcome by the Trinitarian event in which God gave His Son
> into lostness in order not to allow man to remain alone in the
> lostness of his being.[36]

The Easter Mystery places the 'Theo-drama' beyond the
opposition of tragedy and comedy. Here is a catastrophe beyond
all disasters, and yet here is a triumph surpassing all happy

---

[34] 'The Ballad of the White Horse', Mackey, p. 216.
[35] *The Collected Works of G. K. Chesterton*, vol. 2, p. 344.
[36] *Elucidations*, English translation by John Riches (London, 1975), p. 56.

endings. According to Balthasar, in antiquity it was Greek tragedy rather than philosophy which was the great 'cipher' of Christ, but in Christianity, now that the Only-begotten of the Father has tasted and conquered death in the flesh, there can be no place for a tragedy of 'absolute gravity'.[37] Tragedy cannot be the dominant note in Christian literature. As Balthasar says in *Herrlichkeit*:

> It is no accident that, in Christian literature, comedy on the whole outweighs tragedy. In Shakespeare the two are finely balanced, but in the English novel right up to Chesterton, it is humour which increasingly has the upper hand. Molière has more penetration than Racine, Goldoni more weight than Alfieri. In Austria, with Mozart, Raimund, Nestroy, Hofmannsthal, Christian light triumphs over bogus German gravity ... I am talking about the light of humour, for irony presumes to take on the perspective of God, while the pharisaism of satire sits in judgement (accusingly or leniently) on the faults of one's neighbour ... By contrast, the Christian humorist knows about the mysterious relationship between the wisdom of grace and the folly of sin and the abyss between them, at once open and closed.[38]

With similar insight, Chesterton notes how often the great Christian martyrs have been blessed with the grace of gentle good humour, thus proving that theirs is a transformed tragedy, a little pain held within the great pain of the God-Man. He loved the fact that the missionary priest St John Kemble died smoking 'in spite of the fury which faddists like James the First were to fulminate against tobacco'.[39] Above all, he revered and revelled in the memory of St Thomas More:

> Behind his public life, which was so grand a tragedy, there was a private life that was perpetual comedy ... Everybody knows, of course, that the comedy and the tragedy met, as they meet in Shakespeare, on that last high wooden stage where his drama ended.[40]

---

[37] *Herrlichkeit. Eine theologische Ästhetik*, vol. 3/1, Im Raum der Metaphysik (Einsiedeln, 1965), pp. 94ff.

[38] Ibid., p. 504.

[39] *Chaucer*, p. 300. G. K. gets his dates wrong. St John Kemble died in 1679, long after the death of James the First.

[40] *The Well and the Shallows*, in *The Collected Works of G. K. Chesterton*, vol. 3, p. 508.

The poet Francis Thompson gives us perhaps the best account of all of the meeting of tragedy and comedy in the life of More. It is fitting to make mention of Thompson here, first because he was admired by both Balthasar and Chesterton,[41] and secondly, because, alongside Claudel, Péguy, and St Thérèse, he is one of the outstanding prophets of Christian hope during the 'Nihilistic Nineties'.

> To the keen *accolade* and holy
> Thou didst bend low a sprightly knee,
> And jest Death out of gravity
> As a too sad-visaged friend;
> So, jocund, passing to the end
> Of thy laughing martyrdom;
> And now from travel art gone home
> Where, since gain of thee was given,
> Surely there is more mirth in Heaven.[42]

3. The Catholicity of the Truth

The word 'Catholic' means 'whole', and so the Catholic faith is the faith in its fulness, the whole faith and nothing but the faith. By contrast, the heresies are so many subtractions, selections, and removals from the beautiful whole. Precisely as form, as beautiful, Divine Revelation has integrity, one of the defining attributes of beauty according to St Thomas. The heretic is, therefore, always an iconoclast (who, as Chesterton once observed, is 'the lowest of all the unskilled trades'):[43] by shattering truth's integrity, he robs it of its radiance. Only orthodoxy, full and right belief, has full and right glory.

This is another matter on which Balthasar explicitly confesses himself to be of one mind with Chesterton. H.U. says of G.K. that he is someone who 'romps without care' in the 'fulness

---

[41] Balthasar uses a long quotation from Thompson as an epigraph at the beginning of the second volume of *Herrlichkeit*. Chesterton expresses his admiration for Thompson on a number of occasions (e.g. in *The Victorian Age in Literature* [New York, 1913], pp. 202f.).

[42] 'To the English Martyrs' in *The Poems of Francis Thompson*, new edition (London, 1913), p. 285.

[43] *The Daily News* (26 April 1905).

and many-sidedness of the truth ... without feeling any necessity to give to this fulness any other than a paradoxical expression'.[44] That is not quite fair. Chesterton does much more than affirm the fulness of the faith through paradoxes. He also shows the disastrous consequences of the selections and imbalances of heresy. As he says in his *Autobiography*:

> I have found only one creed that could not be satisfied with a truth, but only with the Truth, which is made of a million such truths and yet is one ... If I had wandered away like Bergson or Bernard Shaw, and made up my own philosophy out of my own precious fragment of truth, merely because I had found it for myself, I should soon have found that truth distorting itself into a falsehood.[45]

As an example of what happens to a truth when it is wrenched from its place within the Catholic whole, Chesterton most regularly cites Calvinism. In *The Catholic Church and Conversion*, he writes:

> [A] Calvinist is a Catholic obsessed with the Catholic idea of the sovereignty of God. But when he makes it mean that God wishes particular people to be damned, we may say with all restraint that he has become a rather morbid Catholic. In point of fact he is a diseased Catholic; and the disease left to itself would be death or madness. But as a matter of fact, the disease did not last long, and is itself now practically dead. But every step he takes back towards humanity is a step back towards Catholicism.[46]

In *Das Ganze im Fragment*, Balthasar calls Chesterton as a witness to defend the proposition that to make extractions from the Catholic totality of Divine Revelation is self-defeating. Something monstrous happens when men attempt to use Christian 'ideas' without accepting in faith all of Christian revelation. The part can only live and be healthy when incorporated within the whole.

---

[44] *Herrlichkeit*, vol. 2, Fächer der Stile, part 1, Klerikale Stile, p. 19.
[45] *Autobiography*, p. 351.
[46] *The Catholic Church and Conversion* (New York, 1926), pp. 80f.

Chesterton was right when he said that the world is full of Christian ideas gone mad. The Gospel and the Church are plundered like a fruit tree, but the fruits, once separated from the tree, go rotten and are no longer frutiful. The 'ideas' of Christ cannot be separated from Him, and so they are of no use to the world unless they are fought for by Christians who believe in Christ, or at least by men who are inwardly, though unconsciously, open to Him and governed by Him. Radiance is only possible when the radiant centre is permanently active and alive. There can be no shining from stars long dead.[47]

Truth, says Balthasar, using a metaphor that comes from the Church Fathers,[48] is 'symphonic'. The divinely revealed truth taught by the Catholic Church is neither raucous cacophony nor rigid unison, but rather rich polyphony, the harmonious richness of the resounding Word made flesh.[49] Chesterton uses the same image. The trouble with the modernist, he says, is that the poor man has only one note to play. He has discarded the full score which Christ has given His Church.

> It is the musical instrument of the Modernist that has broken all its strings but one, like the lute in the agnostic picture of Hope; and continues to strike the same few chords of truth remaining to it, but drearily and all on one note.[50]

The heretic's choice of the part to the neglect of the whole is, as the Church's Tradition has always recognized, a species of pride. Chesterton says that it is a kind of snobbery, a lazy assertion of self against the demanding wisdom of Christ's Bride.

---

[47] Balthasar, *Das Ganze im Fragment*, pp. 198f.

[48] St Ignatius of Antioch, for example, urges the faithful of the Ephesian Church to be of one mind with their bishop and clergy: 'Form yourselves, each and all, into a choir, that, being harmonious in concord (*symphônoi ... en homonoia*) and taking the tone from God, you may sing with one voice to the Father through Jesus Christ' (*Epistula ad Ephesios*, n. 4, in *The Apostolic Fathers*, part 2, vol. 2, section 1, J. B. Lightfoot, ed. [London, 1885], pp. 41f).

[49] *Die Wahrheit ist symphonisch. Aspekte des christlichen Pluralismus* (Einsiedeln, 1972), p. 7.

[50] *The Well and the Shallows*, in *The Collected Works of G. K. Chesterton*, vol. 3, p. 420.

It is always easy to let the age have its head; the difficult thing is to keep one's own. It is always easy to be a modernist, as it is easy to be a snob.[51]

4. The Adventure of Authority

To the surprise of an Edwardian age complacent in its theological liberalism, Chesterton announced that Christian orthodoxy is an exhilarating adventure, whereas heresy is in every case a dull confinement of the mind. Orthodoxy is adventurous because it is emancipating; it is truth, and truth, the truth of Christ, sets us free. This insight was eventually to lead Chesterton into the Catholic Church. Far from being a prison, the Catholic Church has the spaciousness and liberty of a palace.

> [W]hen he has entered the Church, he finds that the Church is much larger inside than it is outside. He has left behind him the lop-sidedness of lepers' windows and even in a sense the narrowness of Gothic doors; and he is under vast domes as open as the renaissance and as universal as the Republic of the world. He can say, in a sense unknown to all modern men, certain ancient and serene words: *Romanus civis sum*; I am not a slave.[52]

The Church teaches with Christ's authority, His truth lives in her, and so her Magisterium frees a man from everything that enslaves his reason – the delusions of the world, the lies of the devil, the fads and fancies of his own mind.

> The Catholic Church is the only thing which saves a man from the degrading slavery of being a child of his age ... We do not really want a religion that is right where we are right. What we want is a religion that is right where we are wrong.[53]

According to Balthasar, in statements such as these, Chesterton expounds part of the thesis of Balthasar's own *Theodramatik*: the history of salvation is a drama, the dramatic interplay of infinite and finite freedom.

[51] Chesterton, *Orthodoxy*, p. 186.
[52] *The Catholic Church and Conversion*, p. 64.
[53] Ibid., pp. 93–95.

Characteristically, the insight that God freely created the world and endowed it with freedom forms the turning-point of Chesterton's conversion, resulting in a change to a dramatic view of existence. Having tried the modern immanentist world views – materialism, idealism, evolutionism – which caused him to swing back and forth like a pendulum from extreme optimism to extreme pessimism, he experienced this illumination: 'According to most philosophers, God in making the world enslaved it. According to Christianity, in making it, He set it free. God had written, not so much a poem, but rather a play; a play He had planned as perfect, but which necessarily had been left to human actors and stage-managers, who had since made a great mess of it.'[54]

As for the liberating character of the Church's teaching, this is one of the major themes of Balthasar's ecclesiology:

The Church asserts herself only in order to liberate people; she defines only to confront them with the *mysterium*; she does not compel them by magic but takes the risk of exercising her office, trusting in the free assent of her believers. Chesterton illustrates this in a paradoxical, joyous way: 'The outer ring of Christianity is a rigid guard of ethical abnegations and professional priests; but inside that inhuman guard you will find the old human life dancing like children and drinking wine like men; for Christianity is the only frame for pagan freedom. But in the modern philosophy the case is opposite; it is its outer ring that is obviously artistic and emancipated; its despair is within.'[55]

'Why', asks Balthasar, 'do I remain in the Church?' His answer is worthy of Chesterton: 'Because it is the only chance

[54] *Theodramatik*, vol. 2, part 1, Der Mensch in Gott (Einsiedeln, 1976), p. 171n.
[55] Chesterton, *Orthodoxy*, cited by Balthasar in *Der antirömische Affekt*, p. 221. In another place, Balthasar mentions how Claudel, in his correspondence with J. Rivière, quoted Chesterton's *Orthodoxy* to the effect that the Catholic *via media* is not a dull middle-of-the-road position: 'Christian truth differs from all other doctrines in that it does not find wisdom in a kind of mediocre neutrality, but in apparently contradictory opinions, which always seem to be pushed to the furthest extreme: joy and penance, pride and humility, love and renunciation etc. As if stretched upon a cross, man experiences its extreme tension and stretching power in all directions ... That was the great watchword of Christian art and culture and made of Europe something very different from this ridiculous "kingdom of the centre"' (*Das Ganze im Fragment*, p. 251n).

to escape from oneself, from this curse of one's importance, of one's own gravity.'[56] The man who is orthodox, the Christian content to be faithful to His Mother the Church, begins to reflect the largeness of her mind and heart. As Balthasar liked to say, following Origen and St Ambrose, such a man is an 'ecclesiastical soul',[57] holy, catholic, and apostolic.

II. Chesterton in Balthasar, Balthasar in Chesterton

1. The Child with the Mother

A very Chestertonian surprise awaits the reader of the first part of the third volume of *Herrlichkeit*. It is an immense and amazing structure: this mere 'first part' consists of nearly a thousand pages. We are 'in the realm of metaphysics', and all mankind's poets and philosophers throng the kingdom's vast castle, each ready to show us his perception of being's beauty, the splendour of the real. Homer and Hesiod open the gate. Plato, Virgil, and Plotinus await us in the front parlour. St Augustine and St Thomas lead us up the stairs, towards a promise of the stars. There are distractions to right and left. Saints and holy fools guide us higher; nominalists and rationalists pull us down. We are welcomed by Hölderlin and Goethe, harassed by Hegel and Marx. Finally, we reach the highest room in the house, the last chapter, the pinnacle of Balthasar's achievement as a Christian philosopher. We open the door marked 'The Place of Glory in Metaphysics' and find ... a woman with her baby. Being is glorious, and the first to perceive the glory is the child when he sees his mother smile. The newborn baby, Balthasar argues, is the primal metaphysician.

> Of course, the child does not awaken into consciousness with this question in his mind. And yet it lies, unacknowledged but alive, in the first opening of his mind's eyes. His 'I' awakens with his experience of the 'Thou'. In his mother's smile he learns that he is

---

[56] *Elucidations*, p. 215.

[57] On the notion of the *anima ecclesiastica*, see Balthasar, 'Wer ist die Kirche?' in *Sponsa Verbi*. Skizzen zur Theologie 3 (Einsiedeln, 1961), pp. 174ff.

affirmed and loved, that he has been admitted to something incomprehensibly all-encompassing, an already existing reality which shelters and nourishes him.[58]

Existence is marvellous, being is lovely; in fact, being is the gift of love, as Balthasar says, quoting Angelus Silesius:

> Being comes from love, and even the countenance of God
> Has its loveliness from love, or else it would not shine.[59]

Everything comes together here: Plato and Aristotle, who held that wonder was the beginning of philosophy, Virgil with the mysterious prophecy of the Fourth Eclogue (*Incipe, parve puer, risu cognoscere matrem*), indeed all who have marvelled at being through the ages. All the wisdom of the poets and philosophers is gathered together, but it is also raised up, because it is taken up by the Gospel, by the One who said that 'Unless you turn and become like children, you will never enter the Kingdom of Heaven' (Matt. 18:3). Balthasar writes:

> The Christian is the guardian of the metaphysical wonder with which philosophy begins, and in whose permanence it carries on its work ... Christians today, living as they do in a night deeper than that of the late Middle Ages, have been given the task of affirming being, untroubled by the darkness and distortion. This act of affirmation is to be performed vicariously and representatively on behalf of all mankind.[60]

This statement of Balthasar's is profoundly Chestertonian; indeed, it expresses a central theme of Chesterton's *Autobiography*, even of his whole work. Chesterton, like Balthasar, believed that the main point of the activities of philosophers and artists was 'to dig for [the] submerged sunrise of wonder, so that a man sitting in a chair might understand that he was actually alive, and be happy'.[61] Simply to exist is wonderful, God's first gift, and, unless the wickedness of men frustrate him, no one has more natural capacity to enjoy the gift or sense the wonder than the child. The child does not normally walk

---

[58] *Herrlichkeit. Eine theologische Ästhetik*, vol. 3/1, Im Raum der Metaphysik, p. 945.

[59] Ibid., p. 975.

[60] Ibid., p. 976.

[61] *Autobiography*, p. 91.

around in a kind of 'dazed day-dream'; no, it is *things* which he finds wonderful; he loves the splendour of the real.[62] This simple truth, the first truth of all art, philosophy, and religion, the Church now has to defend ever more bravely and loudly as the world plunges further into the civilization of death.

We poor tired sons of Adam need to be made young again. We have to turn and become like children. We have to recapture the wonder. But we cannot do so by the techniques of psychology, nor indeed by any unaided human effort. Men have to be reborn 'from above'. They can only become children by the grace of the God who for them became a child, the Child of the Blessed Virgin Mary. This was the subject of Balthasar's very last book, *Wenn Ihr nicht werdet wie dieses Kind*.[63] It is also the theme of many of Chesterton's greatest poems:

> Hark! Laughter like a lion wakes
> To roar to the resounding plain,
> And the whole Heaven shouts and shakes,
> For God Himself is born again,
> And we are little children walking
>   Through the snow and rain ...

> Have a myriad children been quickened,
> Have a myriad children grown old,
> Grown gross and unloved and embittered
> Grown cunning and savage and cold?
> God abides in a terrible patience,
> Unangered, unworn,
> And again for the child that was squandered
>   A child is born.[64]

'Everywhere outside Christianity', says Balthasar, 'the child is automatically sacrificed'.[65] Pagan antiquity saw the child as

[62] 'Now children and adults are both fanciful at times; but that is not what, in my mind and memory, distinguishes adults from children. Mine is a memory of a sort of white light on everything, cutting things out very clearly, and rather emphasizing their solidity. The point is that the white light had a sort of wonder in it, as if the world were as new as myself; but not that the world was anything but a real world' (ibid., pp. 42f).

[63] Stuttgart, 1988.

[64] 'The Wise Men' and 'The Nativity', Mackey, pp. 129, 139.

[65] *Das Ganze im Fragment*, p. 282.

property and possession, some*thing* that was incompletely human. The Promethean ideologies of the modern age repeat the same terrible error. Balthasar agrees with Bernanos that the child – and the spirit of the child – is the chief victim of de-christianized modern western culture. 'Human society is built upon the tacit, thousandfold murder of the unborn.'[66]

Christianity alone truly cherishes the child. 'Only in the mystery of the Word made flesh', say the Fathers of the Second Vatican Council, 'is the mystery of man made clear.' 'Only in the light of God-made-child', we may add, 'can human beings fully understand and finally recover their childhood.' In the words of Balthasar:

> It took the Incarnation of Christ to show the eternal significance, theological and not just anthropological, of being born, the utter blessedness of coming forth from a life-conceiving, life-bearing womb.[67]

Why is revelation necessary to bring home to man the meaning and value of his own early days? Because his intellect has been weakened and wounded by the sin of his first father. There are truths concerning man's nature, in principle knowable by reason, which in his fallen condition he finds it hard to grasp: the dignity of childhood is one of these. As Balthasar says:

> Everything said here about the human child is part of human existence, and so it is not really an object of God's self-revelation in Jesus Christ. Nevertheless, much of what is deepest in man, because of his alienation from God, is submerged and forgotten. Only through the Incarnation is it brought back to the light of remembrance and human self-understanding. In our case this takes place through Jesus' teaching about the indispensability of the truly childlike attitude if we are to share in the Kingdom of God, which He has brought near.[68]

The blessing brought by the Babe of Bethlehem, the fruit of Christmas, Easter, and Pentecost, is the gift of a new childhood

---

[66] Ibid., p. 276.
[67] 'Das Kind Jesu und die Kinder', *Homo creatus est*. Skizzen zur Theologie, vol. 5 (Einsiedeln, 1986), p. 173.
[68] *Wenn Ihr nicht werdet wie dieses Kind*, p. 18.

in Him. In the Sacrament of Baptism we are given second birth, the grace of sonship in the Son, and then, in the Sacrament of Penance, the risen Jesus rejuvenates us out of the aging ravages of sin. In Chesterton's words:

> [The Catholic] believes that in that dim corner, and in that brief ritual, God has really remade him in His own image. He is now a new experiment of the Creator. He is as much a new experiment as he was when he was really only five years old. He stands ... in the white light at the worthy beginning of the life of a man. The accumulations of time can no longer terrify. He may be grey and gouty, but he is only five minutes old.[69]

Only in Christianity, only in Christ, is the poet's yearning for a new childhood fulfilled. *O dass ich lieber wäre wie Kinder sind*, 'Were only I as children are!', cried Hölderlin in the night of his madness. The Child of the Virgin Mary answers that prayer, as Balthasar says in *Das Ganze im Fragment*:

> Now the backward glance to lost childhood – as cultivated by Christian poets – is no longer just a romantic dream, but a longing for a lost innocence and intimacy with God that Jesus and Mary never lost, and which through the depths of the grace of Baptism and the ever-renewed forgiveness of sins always lies before us. Only the Christian view of the mystery of childhood can offer a counter-weight to the heedlessness of the delusion of progress, whether it appears in anti-Christian or neutral, or even Christian guise.[70]

2. The Mother with the Child

The Magi found the Child Jesus with Mary His Mother (cf. Matt. 2:11), and so do we. It is not human childhood in isolation that is exalted by the Incarnation of the Son of God, but childhood and motherhood together. As Balthasar says:

> The Madonna and Child are, for the Christian, the unique, incomparable pair which places every mother and child relationship within the radiance of eternal grace.[71]

---

[69] *Autobiography*, p. 341.
[70] *Das Ganze im Fragment*, pp. 282f.
[71] Ibid., p. 270.

We cannot hope to be led by the divine Lamb or learn from Him if we turn away from the human Mother He deigned to share with us. Sadly, Protestantism would not accept the gift of the Blessed Mother, and, by a terrible inevitability, the Maryless Christology became a Christianity without Christ. Already in the nineteenth century, in the early decades of Liberal Protestantism, Cardinal Newman pointed to the tragic irony of the fact that the religion which once threw off devotion to Our Lady in order to give more glory to her Son had now ended up by refusing to worship Him as God.[72]

In *The Everlasting Man*, Chesterton illustrates from his own memory the strange deformity that comes upon Christianity when Christians will not honour the woman in whose flesh and by whose faith God became man. He writes as follows:

> When I was a boy a more Puritan generation objected to a statue upon my parish church representing the Virgin and Child. After much controversy, they compromised by taking away the Child. One would think that this was even more corrupted with Mariolatry, unless the Mother was counted less dangerous when deprived of a sort of weapon. But the present difficulty is also a parable. You cannot chip away the statue of a mother from all round that of a newborn child ... Similarly, you cannot suspend the idea of a newborn child in the void or think of him without thinking of his mother. You cannot visit the child without visiting the mother; you cannot in common human life approach the child except through his mother. If we are to think of Christ in this aspect at all, the other idea follows as it is followed in history. We must either leave Christ out of Christmas, or Christmas out of Christ, or we must admit, if only as we admit in an old picture, that those holy heads are too near together for the haloes not to mingle and cross.[73]

Balthasar has his own beautiful metaphor to enunciate the same truth. He speaks of 'the Christological Constellation'. Christ, the Sun of Justice, the central star, shines with an

[72] Cf. the meditation on Our Lady as 'Tower of David' in John Henry Cardinal Newman, *Prayers, Verses, and Devotions* (San Francisco, 1989), pp. 170f.

[73] *The Everlasting Man*, in *The Collected Works of G. K. Chesterton*, vol. 2, pp. 169f.

incomparable splendour, but He does not shine alone.[74] In Heaven, as once on earth, He is inseparable from His Blessed Mother and gives us all His graces through her. The Mother / Son relationship is indestructible.

> At the beginning, at the very heart of the Incarnation event, stands Mary, the perfect Handmaid, who 'let it be done unto her'. She consented both physically and spiritually to a motherly relationship with the person and work of her Son. This relationship might change as Jesus grew and developed His independent personality, but it would never be extinguished.[75]

Balthasar warned on many occasions of the terrible consequences of taking the Child from His Mother.

> Without Mariology Christianity threatens imperceptibly to become inhuman. The Church becomes functionalistic, soulless, a hectic enterprise without any point of rest, estranged from its true nature by the planners. And because, in this manly-masculine world, all that we have is one ideology replacing another, everything becomes polemical, critical, bitter, humourless, and ultimately boring, and people in their masses run away from such a Church.[76]

All the gifts of the Redeemer – the grace of Christian good humour, the virtue of childlike hope, the exhilaration of orthodoxy – pass through the love and prayers of Our Lady, the Mediatrix of All Graces. That is why, for the two great men I have been discussing, she somehow sums up in her person the whole of Catholic Christianity. The Queen of Heaven brings everything down to earth. As Chesterton says:

> Our Lady, reminding us especially of God Incarnate, does in some degree gather up and embody all those elements of the heart and the higher instincts, which are the legitimate short cuts to the love of God.[77]

---

[74] Balthasar unfolds the metaphor of the 'Christological Constellation' in *Der antirömische Affekt*, pp. 115ff. See my essay 'Mary and Peter in the Christological Constellation: Balthasar's Ecclesiology' in John Riches, ed., *The Analogy of Beauty. The Theology of Hans Urs von Balthasar* (Edinburgh, 1986), pp. 105–133.

[75] *Der antirömische Affekt*, pp. 116f.

[76] Balthasar, *Elucidations*, p. 72.

[77] *The Well and the Shallows*, in *The Collected Works of G. K. Chesterton*, vol. 3, p. 40.

Balthasar always sees the Church in Mary and Mary in the Church. She is not only the Church's model and Mother, but also in some way the Church's personification.[78] She is the *Kirche im Ursprung*, the Church's immaculate beginning as well as her glorious final destiny.[79] In words which show both the humility of a child and the chivalry of a knight, Chesterton likewise explains in *The Well and the Shallows* how Our Lady and the Catholic Church were always in his mind bound up together:

> I never doubted that this figure was the figure of the Faith; that she embodied, as a complete human being still only human, all that this Thing had to say to humanity. The instant I remembered the Catholic Church, I remembered her; when I tried to forget the Catholic Church, I tried to forget her; when I finally saw what was nobler than my fate, the freest and the hardest of all my acts of freedom, it was in front of a gilded and very gaudy little image of her in the port of Brindisi, that I promised the thing that I would do, if I returned to my own land.[80]

These words require no commentary, nor does my already long tale of these unlikely likenesses need lengthening. We have arrived at the main connection. Now at last we know why the likeness between Balthasar and Chesterton is greater than the differences. A common maternal influence kept their souls youthful unto death. By the intercession of Virgin Mother Mary, and through the Sacraments of Virgin Mother Church, the Holy Spirit renewed them in the likeness of the Lamb and moved them to tread His little way to the Father. There was a family resemblance. Balthasar and Chesterton are sons of the same Mother.

[78] On Our Lady as 'Woman for Christ and Church', see Balthasar, *Theodramatik*, vol. 2, Die Personen des Spiels, part 2, Die Personen in Christus (Einsiedeln, 1978), pp. 276ff.

[79] See my article 'Mary and Peter in the Christological Constellation' (note 69 above). The phrase *Maria – Kirche im Ursprung* is used by Balthasar and Cardinal Ratzinger as the title of their little book on Our Lady (Freiburg, 1981).

[80] *The Well and the Shallows*, in *The Collected Works of G. K. Chesterton*, vol. 3, p. 462.

Postscript

And a great sign appeared in Heaven: a Woman clothed with the sun and the moon under her feet, and on her head a crown of twelve stars. And being with child, she cried travailing in birth, and was in pain to be delivered. And there was seen another sign in Heaven. And behold a great red dragon, having seven heads and ten horns and on his heads seven diadems . . . And the dragon stood before the Woman who was ready to be delivered, that, when she should be delivered, he might devour her son. And she brought forth a man child, who was to rule all nations with an iron rod. And her son was taken up to God and to His throne. And the woman fled into the wilderness, where she had a place prepared by God, that there they should feed her, a thousand two hundred sixty days.

(Apoc. 12:1–6)

The Dragon is poised to attack the Child of the Woman, but the Woman and her Child overcome him. This Woman, whom John saw shining in the Apocalypse, is the Woman Moses saw shadowed in Genesis (cf. Gen. 3:15). She is the Ever-Virgin Mother of God, the New Eve, the Woman who mediates with the Mediator (cf. John 2:4) and co-operates with the work of the Redeemer (cf. John 19:26). Here John catches sight of her as the glorious Lady of the Assumption. The sun that clothes her is the risen splendour of Christ the Sun of Righteousness, the radiance He poured out upon her when He took her, soul and body, into His Father's house in Heaven.[1] But the Woman

---

[1] According to St Bonaventure, Our Lady is clothed with 'the light of eternal radiance' (cf. *De annuntiatione Beatae Virginis Mariae sermo* 4, 1; *Sancti Bonaventurae opera omnia*, vol. 9 [Quaracchi, 1901], p. 672), the 'beauty of the Sun of Righteousness' (*De assumtione Beatae Virginis Mariae sermo* 2, 2; ibid., p. 692).

clothed with the sun is also the Church Triumphant on the last day, of whose glory *Maria assumpta* is the 'image and beginning'.[2] And the Woman is every woman, all the daughters of the Old Eve, and the sun is the honour done to their womanhood through God's choice of the Virgin to be His Blessed Mother.[3]

The moon under the Woman-Mary's feet is the Church, which is a moon in relation to Christ, brilliant with His reflected light.[4] The Church is placed beneath Our Lady in the sense that Our Lady is the Mother of the Church and the pre-eminent member of the Church, the Church's 'mediatrix with the Sun of Righteousness'.[5] The moon under the Woman-Church's feet is the waxing and waning moon of worldly wisdom, which is foolishness to God (cf. Ecclus. 27:12; 1 Cor. 1:20).[6] The Church preaches Eternal Wisdom Crucified, which is foolishness to the world (cf. 1 Cor. 1:18ff.). The moon under the feet of Everywoman is the same mad wisdom of the world in its contempt for true womanhood: the receptivity which is the natural mark of femininity and the 'communion with the mystery of life' which is the glory of maternity.[7] The twelve stars on Our Lady's head are the Twelve Patriarchs, the Fathers of the Hebrews, of whom Mary of Nazareth is the fairest daughter, 'the joy of Israel . . . the honour of our people' (cf. Judith 15:10). The twelve stars on the head of the Church Triumphant are the totality of the saints, that is to say, the multiplication of those who, from the four corners of the earth, have had living faith in the Three-Personed God. The twelve stars on the head of the Church Militant are the twelve Apostles and all who share their ministry in the Church. This masculine priesthood, acting in the person of the 'man child' Christ, is at the chivalrous

[2] Cf. *Lumen gentium*, n. 68.

[3] 'Mary is the "new beginning" of the dignity and vocation of women, of each and every woman' (Pope John Paul II, *Mulieris dignitatem*, n. 11).

[4] Cf. St Bernard of Clairvaux, *In dominica infra octavam assumptionis sermo* 3, 5; J. Leclercq OSB and H. Rochais, eds., *Sancti Bernardi opera*, vol. 5 (Rome, 1968), p. 265.

[5] Ibid., n. 15, p. 274.

[6] Ibid., n. 3, p. 264.

[7] Cf. Pope John Paul II, *Mulieris dignitatem*, n. 18.

service of the Woman-Church. The twelve stars on the head of Everywoman are the fruits of the Holy Spirit borne by any woman who corresponds with the Spirit's Grace and Gifts.

The Dragon is the Old Serpent, 'who is called the Devil and Satan' (v. 9), and his seven heads are the seven capital sins to which he tempts the children of Eve.[8] The Woman crying out, travailing in birth, is not the Virgin Theotokos in Bethlehem, who brought forth her Son without pain and corruption,[9] but the Virgin Co-redemptrix on Calvary: *cruciabatur ut pareret*, 'she was crucifyingly in pain to be delivered'. By her night of faith, she shared in the dereliction of the Son and co-operated under Him in restoring divine adoption to men. The Woman crying out is also the Church Militant, as she strives, in the face of Satan's fury, to bring forth sons in the likeness of Christ.[10] And the Woman crying out is every woman, every daughter of Eve, despised by the Devil for the receptivity of her femininity and the generosity of her maternity.

The Child is the Christ Child persecuted by the Devil through the instrumentality of King Herod.[11] There was and ever will be enmity between the Serpent's brood and the Woman's Seed (cf. Gen. 3:15).[12] The Child also signifies the children of Mother Church, who can be called collectively a 'man child' because all the members of Christ's Mystical Body are 'one Son' with

[8] Cf. Richard of St Victor, *In Apocalypsim Ioannis*, lib. 4; PL 196. 799D.

[9] 'This cannot be applied literally to Blessed Mary, because just as she conceived without pleasure, so she gave birth without pain' (Haymo of Halberstadt (+ 853), *Expositio in Apocalypsim* 3, 12; PL 117. 1081D–1082A). 'Of course, with the whole Catholic tradition, I believe that [the Blessed Virgin] was spared the physical tortures [of childbirth], which are a consequence of our fallen nature. Those words of Genesis (3:15) could not be addressed to the Immaculate: "In sorrow shalt thou bring forth children" (Gen. 3:16)' (Paul Claudel, *Paul Claudel interroge l'Apocalypse* [Paris, 1952], p. 86).

[10] 'This Dragon stands before the Woman about to give birth, because the Devil attacks Holy Church who longs to give birth to Christ in the fruit of good works. And when she does give birth, he wants to devour her child, because he wants to take Christ from her through the corruption of the works' (Richard of St Victor, *In Apocalypsim Ioannis*, lib. 4; PL 196. 799D–800A).

[11] Cf. Rupert of Deutz, *Commentarium in Apocalypsim*, lib 7, cap. 12; PL 169. 1048C.

[12] Cf. St Bernard of Clairvaux, *In dominica infra octavam assumptionis*, n. 4; p. 265.

Him.[13] The Devil wants to expunge the grace of adoptive sonship from their souls. The Child is also, without doubt, every mother's child.[14] Satan wants to devour him because he knows that, in every age and culture, by the wisdom and love of the Creator, every child is an icon of the Christ Child and a model of the Christian disciple.[15]

The wilderness to which the Woman flees is the wilderness of Egypt, where, safe from Herod's hatred, Our Lady and the Child-God were fed and guarded by St Joseph.[16] The wilderness also symbolizes this present age in which the Church Militant, the New Israel, is fed with the manna of Christ's flesh and guarded by the fiery pillar of the Spirit.[17] And the wilderness is the desert of Christian non-conformity to the world, a desert strangely fruitful for the soul of every woman, as it is for the soul of every man.[18]

The Child taken up to God's throne is the ascended Christ, the victorious Lamb. By His Cross and Resurrection, He has defeated the Dragon, and now, in the very flesh in which He died and rose from the tomb, He sits in glory at the Father's right hand.[19] The Child taken up to God's throne also represents the children of the Church, who have the great hope that where their Head is, they, His members, may also be. And the Child

[13] Cf. Emile Mersch, *The Whole Christ*. The Historical Development of the Doctrine of the Mystical Body in Scripture and Tradition, ET (London, 1949), pp. 414ff.

[14] Cf. Pope John Paul II, *Evangelium vitae*, n. 104.

[15] As Cardinal Newman says, 'childhood is a type of the perfect Christian state' ('The State of Innocence', *Parochial and Plain Sermons*, vol. 5, p. 102).

[16] Cf. Cornelius a Lapide, *Commentaria in Scripturam Sacram*, vol. 21 (Paris, 1966), p. 244.

[17] 'Living in the hope of things eternal, the Church rejoices in the pilgrimage of this present desert. She has received power to tread upon serpents and scorpions and all the might of the Red Dragon, as were the People of Israel, who were fed with heavenly bread in the desert and, by the sight of the bronze serpent, overcame the fiery serpents' (St Bede the Venerable, *Explanatio Apocalypsis*, lib. 2; PL 93. 167A).

[18] On the symbolism of the desert, see Louis Bouyer, *The Spirituality of the New Testament and the Fathers*, ET (London, 1960), ch. XIII.

[19] 'This Child is taken up to God and to His throne, because in His humanity He ascends into Heaven, and sits with the Father, and rules and judges the world' (Richard of St Victor, *In Apocalypsim Ioannis*, lib. 4; PL 196. 800A).

taken up to God's throne is all human childhood objectively raised up to a marvellous new dignity through the human childhood of the Father's eternal Son. Only in Baptism will individual children be incorporated into Christ, but already, by the fact of His Incarnation, their childhood has a fresh grandeur and renown.

For the the the sake of every mother's child, the Virgin's Child has conquered. He has cast out the accuser of His brethren.[20] Even now He reigns as the slain Lamb (cf. Apoc. 5:9), carrying the marks of the Passion in His risen flesh as an unfailing supplication of mercy. His Sacrifice once offered on the Cross is not locked away in the past but daily renewed on His Church's altars, and its saving power is applied to the healing of men and the harrowing of Hell. Through the teaching and Sacraments of His Catholic Church, and by the intercession of His Blessed Mother, the Lamb-Shepherd feeds His lambs and leads them to the fountains of life (cf. John 21:15; Apoc. 7:17). Every child has someone on earth to speak for him and defend him. There is a Mother, standing on rock, over whom the child-consuming gates of Gehenna cannot prevail (cf. Matt. 16:18). There is a Mother, a 'valiant woman' (Prov. 31:10), who will crush the head of the Serpent (cf. Gen. 3:15). At the end of the age, through the Woman, Holy Mary and Holy Church, the Father's Lamb will bring His flock into the fold and city of the free (cf. Apoc. 22:14), and the Spirit of the Child will triumph.

And I heard a loud voice in Heaven, saying, 'Now is come salvation and strength and the Kingdom of our God and the power of His Christ, because the accuser of our brethren is cast forth, who accused them before our God day and night. And they overcame Him by the Blood of the Lamb and by the Word of testimony, and they loved not their lives unto death' (Apoc. 12:10–11).

[20] St Bonaventure says that Lucifer was first cast out at his fall, and then he was cast out in a second battle between the good angels and bad 'when the Church was founded in the Passion of Christ, from which the Sacraments derive their power' (De angelis sermo 5; Sancti Bonaventurae opera omnia, vol. 9 [Quaracchi, 1901], p. 630).

ST THÉRÈSE OF LISIEUX

2 January 1873	Marie Françoise Thérèse Martin born in Alençon.
4 January 1873	Baptized in Notre Dame d'Alençon.
1875	At this age Thérèse thinks: 'I will be a religious'.
1876	'From the age of three, I began to refuse nothing of what God asked of me'.
28 August 1877	Mme. Martin dies.
29 August 1877	Mme. Martin is buried. Thérèse chooses Pauline as her second mother.
16 November 1877	The Martin family settle in at Les Buissonnets in Lisieux.
3 October 1881	Enters Benedictine Abbey as a day-girl.
2 October 1882	Pauline enters Lisieux Carmel.
December 1882	Suffers headaches, insomnia, pimples.
25 March 1883	Falls ill at her relatives, the Guérins: trembling, hallucinations.
13 May 1883	Our Lady of the Smile. Thérèse is cured.
8 May 1884	First Holy Communion.
14 June 1884	Confirmation.
15 October 1886	Her sister Marie enters Carmel. Thérèse is delivered from her scruples through the prayers of her four little brothers and sisters who died in infancy.
25 December 1886	Thérèse's 'conversion' at Les Buissonnets. The newborn Christ heals her of her sensitiveness and 'girds her with His weapons'.
29 May 1887	Wins her father's consent to her entering Carmel at the age of 15.
31 August 1887	Through her prayers, Pranzini is converted on the scaffold.
4 November 1887	Departure for Rome with her father and sister Céline.

20 November 1887	At an audience, she asks Pope Leo XIII for permission to enter Carmel.
28 December 1887	Favourable response from Bishop Hugonin.
9 April 1888	Enters Lisieux Carmel.
22 May 1888	Profession of her sister Marie of the Sacred Heart.
28 May 1888	General confession to Father Pichon.
End of June	Sudden deterioration of the health of M. Martin.
10 January 1889	Receives the habit.
12 February 1889	M. Martin hospitalized at Bon Sauveur, Caen.
July 1889	Receives special grace from Our Lady in hermitage of St Mary Magdalene.
1890	Discovers Isaiah's prophecies of the Suffering Servant. Reads works of St John of the Cross.
8–24 September 1890	Is professed and receives the veil.
10 May 1892	M. Martin is brought back to the family home in Lisieux. Thérèse draws on Scripture in her prayers.
20 February 1893	Sister Agnès of Jesus elected prioress. Thérèse is asked to help in the direction of novices.
23 June 1893	Her sister Léonie enters Visitation convent for second time.
21 January 1894	First 'pious recreation' (play). Plays role of Joan of Arc.
29 July 1894	Death of M. Martin.
14 September 1894	Thérèse's sister Céline enters Lisieux Carmel.
December 1894	Mother Agnès, at the suggestion of Sister Marie, orders Thérèse to write her memories of childhood.
1895	Writes Manuscript A of her autobiography.
9 June 1895	Receives 'the grace to understand better than ever how much Jesus desires to be loved'.
11 June 1895	In response, she offers herself as a holocaust to the merciful love of the good God.
17 October 1895	Mother Agnès designates Thérèse to be spiritual sister to the Abbé Bellière, seminarian and future missionary.

24 February 1896	Profession of Céline as Sister Geneviève of St Teresa.
21 March 1896	Mother Marie de Gonzague elected prioress. Thérèse confirmed in her work with novices.
2/3 April 1896	Holy Thursday night/Good Friday morning, first spitting of blood.
5 April 1896	On Easter Sunday, the trial of faith begins.
30 May 1896	Thérèse is given second spiritual brother, Father Roulland.
8 September 1896	Writes Manuscript B.
November 1896	To discover whether it is God's will that she join the Carmel in Hanoi, Thérèse makes a novena to Tonking martyr, Blessed Théophane Vénard. She suffers a serious relapse.
3 June 1897	Mother Marie de Gonzague orders her to continue working on her autobiography: Manuscript C.
8 July 1897	Leaves her cell for the infirmary.
30 July 1897	Receives Extreme Unction.
19 August 1897	Last Holy Communion.
30 September 1897	At the end of a long agony, in the darkest night of faith, St Thérèse cries out: 'Oh, I love Him! . . . My God, I love you!' and dies in an ecstasy of love.
4 October 1897	Buried in Lisieux cemetery.
10 June 1914	Pope St Pius X signs the decree for introduction of her cause.
14 August 1921	Pope Benedict XV promulgates the decree on the heroism of Sister Thérèse's virtues.
29 April 1923	Beatification by Pope Pius XI.
17 May 1925	Canonization by Pope Pius XI. In the evening 500,000 pilgrims in St Peter's Square.
14 December 1927	Declaration as patron, with St Francis Xavier, of all missions and missionaries.
11 July 1937	Blessing of basilica in Lisieux by the future Pope Pius XII.

3 May 1944	St Thérèse is named patroness of France with St Joan of Arc.
June 1944	Lisieux partly destroyed by allied bombing.
1973	Celebration of the centenary of St Thérèse's birth.
1997	Celebration of the centenary of St Thérèse's death.
19 October 1997	Declared by Pope John Paul II to be a Doctor of the Church.

GILBERT KEITH CHESTERTON

29 May 1874	Born on Campden Hill, Kensington.
1887–1892	St Paul's School.
1 July 1890	First meeting of Junior Debating Club, '. . . a sick cloud upon the soul when we were boys together'.
October 1893	Attends lectures at University College, London. Art classes at the Slade.
Summer 1895	Leaves the Slade without a qualification.
1900	Meets Hilaire Belloc. *Greybeards at Play.* *The Wild Knight and Other Poems* Writes for *The Speaker* and the *Daily News.*
28 June 1901	Marries Frances Blogg at Kensington Parish Church.
1904	Meets Father John O'Connor in Yorkshire. First novel *The Napoleon of Notting Hill.*
1905	*Heretics.*
1906	*Charles Dickens.*
1908	*Orthodoxy.*

1909	The Chestertons move to Beaconsfield.
1911	First appearance of Father Brown in *The Innocence of Father Brown*.
1912–1913	Marconi scandal.
1913	His brother Cecil is received into the Catholic Church.
	His play *Magic* opens in London.
	Denounces Mental Deficiency Act.
November 1914–Easter Eve 1915	Physical and mental breakdown.
1917	*A Short History of England.*
1918	Death of his brother Cecil in a military hospital.
1918–1919	Visits Palestine and Italy.
1921	First lecture tour in USA.
30 July 1922	Received into the Catholic Church.
	Eugenics and Other Evils.
1923	*St Francis of Assisi.*
1925	*The Everlasting Man.*
1926	Inaugural meeting of the Distributist League.
	Frances received into the Church.
	The Outline of Sanity.
	The Queen of Seven Swords.
1927	Visit to Poland.
1929	*The Thing.*
1930	*The Resurrection of Rome.*
1930–1931	Visit to USA.
1932	First broadcast for BBC.
	Chaucer.
	Christendom in Dublin.
1933	*St Thomas Aquinas.*
14 June 1936	Death in Beaconsfield.
	Autobiography.

꧁꧂

CHARLES PÉGUY

7 January 1873	Born in Orléans. His father, a carpenter, dies some months later. Brought up by his mother and grandmother.
1885–1891	At Lycée in Orléans. Academic success.
October 1891	Enters Lycée Lakanal in Sceaux. Ceases to practise his faith.
July 1892	Fails entrance examination to École normale supérieure (ENS).
1892–1893	Military service.
1893–1894	At Lycée Sainte-Barbe, for second year of preparation for ENS.
August 1894	Accepted by ENS.
December 1895	Asks for leave of absence from ENS. Returns to Orléans. Learns printing. Founds Socialist group. Writes part of *Jeanne d'Arc*.
25 July 1896	Death of his friend, Marcel Baudouin.
November 1896	Second year of school.
June 1897	Finishes *Jeanne d'Arc*.
August 1897	*De la cité socialiste*: Péguy's first Socialist manifesto.
28 October 1897	Marries Charlotte-Françoise Baudouin, sister of Marcel Baudouin.
November 1897	Third year as undergraduate.
1 May 1898	Opens Socialist bookshop.
August 1898	Fails final examinations in philosophy. Leaves ENS.
November 1898	Begins to write articles.
5 January 1900	Founds *Cahiers de la quinzaine* ('Fortnightly Notebooks'). 229 issues in 15 series.

September 1908	Tells his friend Lotte: 'I have found the faith again . . . I am a Catholic.'
1910	His *annus mirabilis*. *Le mystère de la charité de Jeanne d'Arc*: first manifestation of regained faith. *Notre jeunesse*: Péguy's life has continuity; all along he has tried to be faithful to one mystical ideal. Makes his famous contrast between *mystique* and *politique*.
1911	*Un nouveau théologien M. Fernand Laudet*: Response to Catholic doubts about his regained faith.
22 October 1911	*Le porche du mystère de la deuxième vertu*: Péguy's great themes emerge: joy, hope, spirit of childhood.
1912	*Le mystère des saints innocents*. *La tapisserie de Sainte Geneviève et de Jeanne d'Arc*. *L'argent*. *La tapisserie de Notre Dame*.
1913	*Ève*: Péguy's greatest work in verse. Pilgrimage to Chartres.
August 1914	Lieutenant in 276th Infantry Regiment. Assists at Mass on the feast of the Assumption. By train to Montdidier area. Forced to retreat. Péguy does retreat on foot.
5 September 1914	Killed by a bullet in the forehead on the first day of the Battle of the Marne. Buried with his fallen comrades at the 'Grande tombe' in Villeroy.

❧

GEORGES BERNANOS

20 February 1888	Born in Paris.
1898–1901	Educated by the Jesuits in Paris.
11 May 1899	First Holy Communion. Begins to be afraid of death.
1901–1904	Junior Seminaries in Paris and Bourges.
October 1904– July 1906	College of Sainte-Marie d'Aire-sur-la-Lys (Pas-de-Calais). Reads Balzac, Hugo, Pascal, Zola, Ernest Hello. Letters to the Abbé Lagrange.
1907–1913	Student at the Sorbonne. Supporter of Action Française.
1913–1914	Editor of monarchist weekly in Rouen.
August 1914	Joins the 6th Dragoons. Wounded several times, citations for bravery.
1917–1920	Friendship with Dom Besse OSB.
11 May 1917	Marries Jeanne Talbert d'Arc, direct descendant of St Joan. Six children, three boys, three girls, born between 1918 and 1933.
1919	Begins to work in insurance, to support his family.
March 1926	Publication of his first novel, *Sous le soleil de Satan*. Decides to become a full-time writer. Deeply affected by the Holy See's condemnation of Action Française.
November 1926	Publication of *L'imposture*.
1929	Publication of *La joie*.

1930–1934	Lives on Côte d'Azur.
1931	Begins to work on *Une mauvaise rêve* and *Monsieur Ouine*.
1933	Motor bike accident. To solve financial problems, decides to write detective novels.
1934	Moves to Majorca.
1936	Publication of *Journal d'un curé de campagne*. The novel wins Grand Prix du Roman of the Académie française. Begins work on *Grands cimetières de la lune*. *Écrits de combat* in response to challenges of the times.
20 July 1938	Moves with his family to South America, first Paraguay, then Brazil.
1939	Finishes *Scandale de la vérité*, *Nous autres Français*.
February– May 1940	Finishes last chapter of *Monsieur Ouine*.
18 June 1940	Decides to support the Free France of General de Gaulle.
1942–1944	*Lettre aux Anglais, Le Chemin de la Croix-des-Âmes*. His sons, Yves and Michel, join the Free French forces.
July 1945	Returns to France in response to telegram from General de Gaulle: 'Your place is among us.'
1947–1948	Lives in Tunisia. Articles of this period published in *Français si vous saviez . . .* Meditates on death while working on *Dialogues des carmélites*. Vows he will write a *Vie de Jésus*. Falls ill with cancer.
5 July 1948	Dies in the American Hospital in Neuilly.

HANS URS VON BALTHASAR

12 August 1905	Born in Lucerne, Switzerland. Educated by the Benedictines at Engelberg and Jesuits at Feldkirch. Studies *Germanistik* and Philosophy at universities of Vienna, Berlin, and Zurich.
1925	First article published on 'The Development of the Musical Idea'.
27 October 1928	Awarded doctorate. Dissertation on 'The History of the Eschatological Problem in Modern German Literature'.
31 October 1929	Enters the Society of Jesus.
1929–1931	Novitiate at Feldkirch.
1931–1933	Philosophy at Berchmanskolleg in Pullach near Munich. Contact with Erich Przywara SJ.
1933–1937	Theology at Lyon (Fourvière). Contact with Henri de Lubac SJ.
26 July 1936	Ordained to the priesthood.
1937–1939	Associate editor of the journal *Stimmen der Zeit*. Co-operation with Hugo and Karl Rahner SJ.
Late 1939	Tertianship (including phase of Jesuit formation) in Pullach.
1940–1948	University chaplain at Basel. Dialogue with Karl Barth.
1 November 1940	Receives Adrienne von Speyr (+1967) into the Catholic Church. With her eventually founds a secular institute, the Community of St John.

1950	Leaves the Society of Jesus. Later incardinated in the Swiss Diocese of Chur.
1950–1988	Active in Basel as leader of Community of St John. Publisher and theological writer.
1969	Appointed by Pope Paul VI to International Theological Commission.
1972	Founds with others *Communio: International Theological Review*.
1984	Awarded Pope Paul VI Prize by Pope John Paul II.
1987	Awarded the Wolfgang Amadeus Mozart Prize in Innsbruck.
29 May 1988	Nominated as a Cardinal by Pope John Paul II.
26 June 1988	Dies suddenly in Basel.

Index